PEOPLE OF YELLOWSTONE

STEVE HORAN | **RUTH W. CROCKER**
PHOTOGRAPHY | ESSAYS

Yellowstone National Park is a national treasure recognized throughout the world. Here are some of the people who live and work in this magnificent park. Experience in photographs and true stories how they lead expeditions, collect scientific data, wrangle horses for trail rides, document seismic activity, study wildlife, rescue stranded hikers, teach visitors how to be safe, and do much more throughout the park's 3,468 square miles.

ELM GROVE

Photographs copyright © 2017 Steve Horan

Essays copyright © 2017 Ruth W. Crocker

Book design copyright © 2017 Joss Maclennan

All rights reserved. No part of this book may be reproduced in any form or by any electronic or mechanical means without permission in writing from the publisher, except by a reviewer who may quote brief passages in a review.

978-1-940863-06-1

Published by Elm Grove Press LLC

To request information about our books, write to:
Elm Grove Press, P.O. Box 153, Old Mystic, CT 06372
Or visit us on the web at: **www.elmgrovepress.org**

10 9 8 7 6 5 4 3 2 1

Printed in the United States of America

Table of Contents

Dedication	viii
Acknowledgments	ix
Map of Yellowstone National Park	1
Introduction	2

THE PORTRAITS

Larry Christensen – Park Service volunteer, veteran, former law enforcement officer	4
Stacy Gerths – Wrangler, trail rider	6
Grant Bulltail – Apsaalooke Crow tribal elder	8
Jim Cole – Artist, musician, teacher	10
Lisa, Jane, and Candy – Three harmless Yellowstone National Park employees	12
Dave Lovalvo – Designer and builder of deep-water exploration devices	14
Jett Hitt – Composer, Yellowstone outfitter and trail guide	16
Jeff Henry – Photographer, writer, fishing guide, winter keeper	18
Ashea Mills – Teacher, writer, snow coach driver, tour guide	20
Stephen Edward Cole – U.S. magistrate judge in Mammoth Hot Springs	22
Loretta Ehnes – Backcountry chef, woodstove cooking expert	24
Bob Kisthart – Backcountry ranger, historian	26
Bob Barbee – Former Yellowstone National Park superintendent	28
Joanne MacCartney – Yellowstone National Park maintenance crew member	30
Jim Horan – Hiker, explorer, book distributor	32
Jim and Heidi Barrett – Environmentalists, artists	34
Tom Murphy – World-renowned nature and wildlife photographer	36
Suzanne Lewis – Former Yellowstone National Park superintendent	38
David Todd – Construction crane operator	40
John Salvato – Bell captain at Old Faithful Inn and Snow Lodge, snow coach driver	42
Bob Richard – Yellowstone National Park ranger (retired), guide, author	44
Beth Kreuzer – Backcountry ranger, wildlife advocate, citizen scientist	46
Robert G. Whipple – Yellowstone National Park ranger, engineer, master builder	48

Table of Contents

Reverend Doctor William "Bill" Young – Former resident minister, Mammoth Hot Springs	50
Charissa Reid – Writer, editor, historian, science interpreter	52
Robert "Bob" Smith – Seismologist, geologist, researcher, teacher	54
Jim Evanoff – Environmental protection specialist	56
Jeff Brown – Director of Yellowstone Association, survivor, educator	58
Bridgette Guild – Museum registrar, curator	60
Mike Stevens – Waterfall discoverer, Yellowstone tour guide, author	62
Bill Berg – Founder of CoolWorks.com, an online job board for "jobs in great places"	64
Michael Finley – Formerly Turner Foundation president and park superintendent	66
MerryCline Pickenpaugh – Seasonal park employee, hiker, disc golfer	68
Norm Miller – Hiker, kayaker, educator, preservationist, time traveler	70
Carl Sheehan – Potter, resident artist at Old Faithful Lodge	72
Doug Smith – Project leader for wolf restoration project, biologist, ecologist	74
Erica Foley Trent – Backcountry ranger, U.S. Army veteran	76
Paul Shea – Yellowstone Gateway Museum curator	78
Terry McEneaney – Yellowstone ornithologist, mountaineer	80
Pat Bigelow – National Park Service fishery biologist	82
John Varley – Former director of Yellowstone Center for Resources, fishery biologist	84
Linda Thurston – Yellowstone wolf tracker, biologist	86
Wendy Medina – Recycler, artist, hiker	88
Jack McConnell – Member of the Jenny Lake "Climbing Rangers" mountain rescue team	90
Dan Wenk – Yellowstone National Park superintendent, landscape architect	92
Charles R. Preston, PhD – Wildlife biologist, museum curator, director, educator	94
Margie Fey – National park ranger, aquatic invasive species inspector	96
John King – Dendrochronologist, ecologist	98
Ethan Perry – Farrier, mechanical engineer	100
Vic Sawyer – Master model builder, snow coach driver, hotel and store manager	102
Nicola Grupido – Manager of housekeeping at Lake Lodge, aspiring writer	104
Caroline McClure – Retail sales manager at Lake Hotel gift shop	106
Fred Ersepke – Yellowstone National Park horse department employee	108
Katy Duffy – Yellowstone National Park ranger, educator, raptor specialist	110
Doug Peacock – Vietnam War veteran, writer, naturalist, filmmaker	112

Table of Contents

Craig Mathews – Professional fly-fishing guide, author	114
Bonnie Gafney Whitman – Park ranger, search-and-rescue dog handler, coroner	116
Eleanor "Ellie" Hamilton Povah – Matriarch of the Hamilton family store tradition	118
Pat Povah – Member of Hamilton family store tradition	120
Mimi Matsuda – Former Yellowstone National Park interpretive ranger, naturalist, artist	122
Dave Peterson – Photographer, Yellowstone resident artist, author	124
Timothy Townsend – Canyon District ranger at Canyon Village	126
Bob Coe – Innkeeper at historic Pahaska Tepee	128
Wayne Goutermont – Carpenter, hunting guide	130
Martha Colby – Official Yellowstone National Park musician, cellist, and pianist	132
Harlan Kredit – Yellowstone National Park ranger, award-winning science teacher	134
Bill Chapman – Artist, wrangler, fire guard, pilot	136
Julianne Baker – Naturalist, educator, former National Park Service ranger	138
Brett Miller – Founder and director of Warfighters Outfitters, combat veteran	140
Rick McIntyre – Biological technician for the Yellowstone wolf project	142
Louisa Willcox – Conservationist, grizzly bear advocate, mountaineer	144
Bob Berry – Author, collector of Yellowstone memorabilia	146
Jim Halfpenny – Naturalist, scientist, educator, author, animal tracker	148
Karen Reinhart – Museum registrar, naturalist, author	150
Steve Blakeley – Transportation dispatcher at Yellowstone National Park	152
Max Brenzel – Auto mechanic, EMT, hiker	154
Wendy Hafer – Helicopter operations specialist for Fire and Rescue	156
Molly Nelson – Civil engineer	158
George Bumann – Sculptor, naturalist, wildlife ecologist, teacher	159
Roger Stradley – Bush pilot, wildlife spotter and tracker	160
Colette Daigle-Berg – Member of Western Montana Search Dogs, retired ranger	162
Warren Johnson – Trail, fishing, and hunting guide; ecologist	164
Will Boekel – Geyser gazer, student	166
Lee Whittlesey – Yellowstone National Park historian, author	168
Salle Engelhardt – Interpretive ranger, artist, musician, former truck driver	170
John J. Craighead – Wildlife advocate and researcher	172
Photographer and Essayist Biographies	174

Dedication

This book is dedicated to all the people who have helped create and preserve Yellowstone National Park since 1872 and all those who will continue this heritage.

Acknowledgments

We are grateful to Steve's brother, Jim Horan, for having the original idea to create a book about people in and around Yellowstone. Jim's home in Livingston, Montana, served as Steve's base camp and nourishment center during the many years he spent pursuing his portrait subjects.

To those who were photographed and who offered their story, we give our heartfelt thanks. It has been an honor to listen to you and work with you.

The book would never have succeeded without Joss Maclennan and her creative spirit and inspired design. Without her vision and talent this project would have been an unfinished dream.

Special thanks go to the Turner Foundation Inc. and its former president, Michael Finley, for support during a crucial time in the project's development. Bravo!!

The scenes behind the making of a book are similar to a busy movie set—lots of folks help to keep things moving. The following people each made unique and important contributions.

Thank you to: Noah Bean, Norman A. Bishop, Timothy P. Bowers, C. J. Box, Donna Brewer, Harriet J. Burns, Clinton Bybee, Tim Cahill, Crystal Cassidy, Larry Christensen, Eljiah Cobb, Lance Craighead, Rachel Cudmore, Kristi Daling, Calvin W. Dunbar, Dale Fowler, Steven Fuller, Carrie Gleason, C. J. Goulding, Jason Hahn, Rick Hoeninghauser, Sam Hollbrook, Alice and Joe Horan, Nina Jaegar, Karin Jones, Beth Kreuzer, Janice Laye, Bud Lilly, Matt Ludin, Rip Mcintosh III, Mike Mease, Norman Miller, Duncan Moran, Dick Perry, Ginger Povah, Penny Preston, Rick Reese, Scott Richardson, Kipp Salle, Jackie Schultz, Aj Scaff, Patty Silversmith, Nathan Varley, Tammy Wert, Kristine Witherspoon, Matthew Wren, John Zumpano.

We appreciate the following organizations for their support, guidance, and generosity:

Arch Venture Partners
Armory Art Centre
Box Gallery
Buffalo Bill Center of the West
Craighead Institute
Cultural Council of Palm Beach County
Delaware North
Elk River Art Gallery
Frame Garden
Future West, Inc.
Livingston Enterprise Newspaper
The town of Livingston, Montana
National Park Service
Palm Beach Photographic Center
Palm Beach Post Newspaper
Turner Foundation Inc.
Yellowstone Gateway Museum
Yellowstone Forever (formerly Yellowstone Association and Yellowstone Park Foundation)
Xanterra Parks and Resorts

Our gratitude to the following individual supporters. Thank you!

Noah Bean, Sheila Block, Michaela Catlin, Larry Christensen, Walter Chruscinski, MerryCline Pickenpaugh, Marco Dib, Gary Elkins, The Esser Family, Lyndsy Fonseca, Douglas Harbert, The Horan Family, Marilyn Kanee, Beth A. Kreuzer, Attiya Khan, Joanne MacCartney, The Maclennan Family, Mimi Matsuda, Norm Miller, Ashea Mills, David Mills, JoAnn & Joel Mowrey, Robin Pacific, Jennifer Beecroft Polishook, John W. Rantala Jr, David Reeves, The Reid Family, Diana H. Rienstra, Hegina Rodrigues.

Map of Yellowstone National Park

Yellowstone National Park was established on March 1, 1872 and is situated above a volcanic hot spot. The park covers almost 3,500 square miles of wilderness. Its dramatic canyons, Alpine rivers, lush forests, hot springs and geysers are predominately in Wyoming, but spread into parts of Montana and Idaho. Seasonal and full-time employees and volunteers work through all seasons to protect the land and its wildlife.

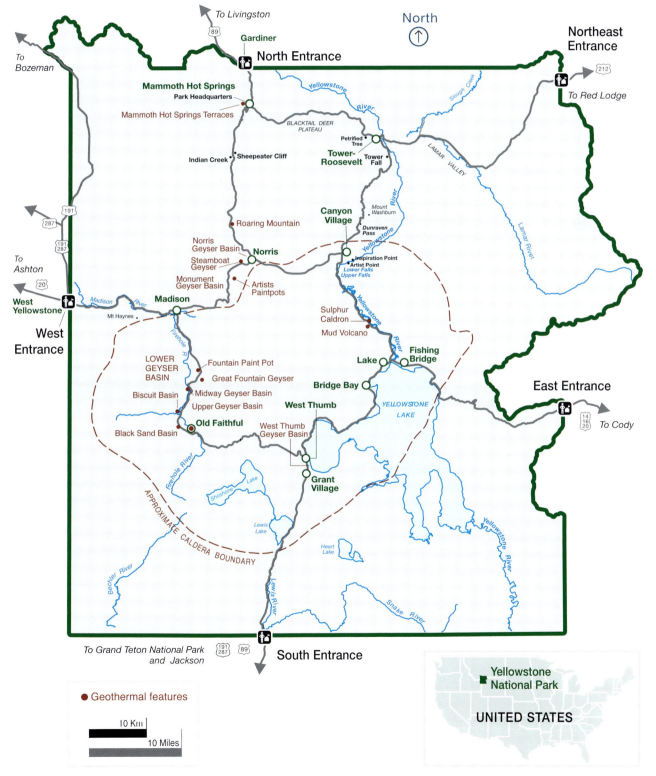

Introduction

Yellowstone National Park is one of the great wonders of the natural world, and preserving it for the future is the work of many individuals who find great joy in what they do. Some are employed by the National Park Service in a variety of jobs, while others work for the concession that operates hotels, restaurants, and stores and provides recreational opportunities for visitors. Still others may be volunteers or work for a private enterprise outside the park boundary. Some people work directly with the almost 4 million visitors who come to Yellowstone each year, while others work behind the scenes to preserve land and wildlife. Ranging from internationally recognized scientists to an outfitter who leads trail rides through the park and composes symphonies inspired by the views, the common theme for all is that they feel fortunate to live and work in such a magnificent place.

Steve Horan first visited Yellowstone in 1984 when his brother, Jim, was employed as a seasonal worker at Roosevelt Lodge, located at the gateway to the magnificent Lamar Valley. Besides the beauty and wildness of the park, Steve was captivated by the *human* nature thriving there, and Jim suggested that Steve capture these interesting people in photographs. Steve had already noticed that the connection among people who work in the park—the friendship and camaraderie and shared sense of purpose—was extraordinary in comparison with other groups of people working together. He discovered that people come to work in Yellowstone from all parts of the U.S. and the world. All seem to have a sense of awe that they have found a way to live, work, and play in Yellowstone country.

Steve was soon convinced that he wanted to create a book of portraits showing these people who are the human connection to this vast and wonderful wild place, the world's first national park. The challenge was to photograph each person at the right moment and in the right place to best show an aspect of their particular story and their special relationship with Yellowstone. He traveled extensively inside the park, always with his camera close at hand, over roads and trails and up and down mountains to meet a range of people as wide as the park's ecosystem: scientists, outfitters, writers, backcountry rangers, naturalists, and road crew—just to name a few. They accommodated him by posing waist deep in icy water, or curling up in an abandoned wolf den, or wading into the Boiling River (which is as hot as its name). He made their horses nervous with light reflectors, or made them wait for Old Faithful to erupt or for the natural light to be exactly right. With the enthusiastic collaboration of each subject, he was relentless in the pursuit of taking each photograph in the perfect place.

By the time Ruth W. Crocker joined the project to conduct interviews and write a brief biography to accompany each photograph, Steve had collected more than one hundred portraits, including one of ranger Bob Whipple, Ruth's brother. Each essay, like the photographs, tells a true story and expresses a personal perspective on what it's like to experience Yellowstone from an "inside" point of view. The essays also reaffirm the almost universal delight and enthusiasm that is exhibited by those who have the privilege to work in and around the park.

In the pages of this book you will meet wranglers; scientists; fish and game experts; Park Service rangers; park superintendents; rescuers who find stranded hikers, climbers, and boaters; guides; historians; environmentalists; wolf and grizzly experts; animal trackers; authors; photographers; bellhops; housekeepers; and many more people with fascinating roles throughout Yellowstone and its environs. Several people within this book discovered Yellowstone country in their youth, often arriving for their first job after high school, and found a place they did not want to leave.

For those who dream—at any age—of living and working in Yellowstone, seeing wild animals and fabulous vistas every day, hiking in primeval forests, discovering waterfalls, or cross-country skiing with a view of wintering bison, this book provides the evidence that these dreams can come true. These photographs and stories capture moments with some successful dreamers who are both enjoying such experiences and also contributing to the preservation of wildness for the benefit of all. Each person featured is making a special and different contribution, but all share the same passion for sustaining Yellowstone and its surrounding ecosystem.

Steve Horan

Ruth W. Crocker

"I love the park, the place, and the events. I feel at home here."

Larry Christensen

National Park Service volunteer, Vietnam War veteran, former law enforcement officer

Spring in Yellowstone! The bison, icon of Yellowstone, begins its birth cycle in mid-April. As the tiny newborn calves are still nursing, they also struggle to keep up with their majestic parents, embarking on the slow migration their ancestors have traveled for more than a thousand years, coming in from the western side of the park.

Their route to summer grazing lands borders the Yellowstone River and may be the same one they have traveled for eons, but today a paved road filled with cars and people competes with the bison migration. Seeing bison on and next to a roadway may be a thrilling sight for visitors, but this is also where troubles often begin.

For several years, Larry Christensen has been there at the confluence where cars, people, and bison meet, to orchestrate the delicate operation of safely herding the bison in their migration. Their movement is slow, less than ten miles a day, hampered by their need to munch new grass and suckle their young. As far as Larry is concerned, they (the bison) are the bosses! "These beautiful creatures can take all the time they want," he says. "This is their land, first."

After Larry retired from a career in law enforcement in 2001, Yellowstone was where he knew he wanted to be. He was fortunate to meet ranger Gary Nelson, who recognized Larry's capacity for managing both people and wild animals. Since then, Larry has felt privileged to be, among other things, a negotiator in the intricate art of untangling elk and bear jams on roadways.

"People stopping their cars in the middle of the road to take a picture can be a big problem," he says. "Other cars can't pass, the animal might decide to approach—and these are wild animals: big, strong creatures who might get cranky."

Larry is a proud recipient of the Master Ranger Corps patch, awarded to those who volunteer in excess of five hundred hours per year and offer a unique service.

His favorite place is with a group of bison, urging them on to their next safe resting spot. "I can stand near a herd and sense what they want to do and read their moods, their snorting and tail twitching. They are the true symbol of America."

Larry recalls growing up in the presence of his Chippewa grandmother in Wisconsin, and perhaps he inherited a spiritual legacy that makes him comfortable among these special animals. Whatever the source of his affinity to the bison, he knows that in Yellowstone, he is "home".

Kindred Spirits: Larry (and friend) on Fountain Flats, Yellowstone National Park.

"Visitors miss a lot in Yellowstone by not getting out of their car."

Stacy Gerths

Wrangler, trail rider

When Big Bear Mom, head wrangler, puts applicants for wrangler jobs through their paces, her selection process is simple but full of intuition. First, she tells each one to saddle up a horse and go for a ride. In Stacy's interview, at age eighteen, she fell off immediately and the horse ran away. "What are you going to do now?" asked Big Bear Mom.

"I guess I'll just get back on another horse," said Stacy, and she was hired.

This was the easy part. Stacy had grown up with horses, but she soon learned that wranglers for Yellowstone National Park trail rides must live, breathe, and eat with horses from 5:00 A.M. until lights-out at 9:00 P.M., with only a half-hour lunch break. Before breakfast, approximately fifty horses have to be saddled, run through a chute, and given a grain bag each morning. After breakfast, it's time to drive the hay truck for supplies and muck out the stalls.

Stacy describes, "Wranglers have to know horses by name along with their temperament and how to keep them calm. Horses need plenty of water or they risk falling. Some horses can't handle a heavier person, and older horses are better with children. The horses know each other, too. When Duchess was matched with Dallas on a ride, she would be very well behaved."

Out on the trail, a wrangler might have to avoid bison or deal with a bluff charge by a bear. Guests on horseback may require some wrangling as well, to encourage them to handle their horse in the safest way and stay aware that they are in wild animal country.

A wrangler's job on a trail ride is to stay aware of how both riders and horses are behaving while watching out for surprises.

But in spite of long, hard days, nothing beats the experience of riding near a herd of elk or beholding the beauty of Cascade meadow or hearing elk and wolves while throwing hay—and working with a manager like Big Bear Mom. "She treated everyone equally and taught us how to protect ourselves and our horses."

"It was the best experience of my life," said Stacy.

Horse Sense: Stacy stands in the Canyon horse corral, where wranglers prepare fifty to sixty horses a day for trail rides in Yellowstone National Park.

"We will bring joy and harmony to everyone we meet."

Grant Bulltail

Apsaalooke Crow tribal elder

Heart Mountain, just north of Cody, Wyoming, rises almost 9,000 feet from the floor of the Bighorn Basin. The rocks on the summit are almost 300 million years older than the rocks at the base, and for more than 100 years geologists have tried to understand how these older rocks came to rest on much younger strata. For Grant Bulltail, tribal elder of the Crow Nation, the "old" resting on the "young" represents the natural order of things. Now in his nineties, he continues to pass down stories of the spirit and traditions of the Apsaalooke ("children of the large-beaked bird") tribe for future generations. The tribe's name was changed to "Crow" by the first Europeans who encountered them in 1743.

Standing in front of Heart Mountain, once part of the vast lands belonging to the Crow, he prays: "To the east for the light of the rising Sun, conveying wisdom, to the south where warm winds blow, toward the north where birds migrate in the summer, and west, where all travel. The land is suffering. We ask that you, the Sun, give them peace," he says, passing a ceremonial pipe among a group gathered to acknowledge and celebrate the spirit of tolerance and collaboration among people.

In one of his many stories about growing up among the Crow people, Grant describes their belief that the pipe was a gift from the Sun, or Maker. They believe that smoking the pipe expels bad energy, empowers the smoker, and restores harmony with nature. The passing of the pipe represents generosity of spirit.

Grant was a small child when Plenty Coups, the last great chief and visionary leader of the Crow Nation, died at age eighty-four in 1932, but he embraced the wisdom of this remarkable peace seeker who wanted the Crow to survive as a people and their customs and spiritual beliefs to be carried on.

He reminds his listeners that the Bighorn and Wind River Basins of north-central Wyoming and southern Montana have been home to Native American tribes for at least 11,000 years.

"We have a long education and we must continue to study, learn, and help one another always. These were the words of Chief Plenty Coups long ago. Our children will carry us into the future."

Man of Peace: Grant wearing the headdress of the Crow Nation.

"Yellowstone is my inspiration in art and song."

Jim Cole

Artist, musician, teacher

Ask any visitor to Yellowstone's Old Faithful Inn in the last thirty years what they remember most besides the geyser erupting like clockwork, and they will possibly tell you that they remember a generous guy dressed in buckskins who gave them a handmade leather key chain and whose rich bass-baritone singing voice could fill the entire inn with everything from Broadway show tunes to songs of the Old West—without a microphone.

When Jim Cole retired from twenty-three years of teaching music to middle school kids, he finally had time to pursue his love of creating art from nature and found objects. But he never stopped singing. It was a natural transition for him to become an official troubadour, serenading visitors from all over the world from the tiny balcony just under the wooden roof of the historic inn. And when he's not performing, he is making and giving to almost everyone he meets creations fashioned from burned leather and other material he has retrieved while hiking along trails outside of the park. (It is forbidden to collect anything within Yellowstone National Park.)

His art studio is a natural history museum filled with furs, hides, and skulls of rare and unusual animals found by him or provided by friends and acquaintances. "My studio is inspired by nature," says Jim. "I've got bobcat, bighorn, black-tailed deer, buffalo, and moose hides with hair. People bring me lots of unusual things. They know I'll like it."

During his "ridin' and ropin'" days he was a familiar face in the Reg Kessler Rodeo, where he jerked open the gate to unleash horses, bulls, and cowboys. Besides singing the national anthem at every Kessler rodeo, he was well known as an expert at bulldogging and cowboy polo. Today he still enjoys horseback riding and backcountry hiking, and he can regale any listener with stories about the migratory habits of northern elk herds or what he likes about winter. But at the heart of everything he does is Jim's love for Montana, Yellowstone, and people. For those lucky enough to meet him as a singer, an artist, a teacher, a natural historian, or a cowboy, they know they have met the true ambassador of Yellowstone.

Artistry with Nature: Jim holds the head of an elk that broke its neck in the fence on Jim's property.

"Can you give us a lift?"

Lisa, Jane, and Candy

Three harmless Yellowstone National Park employees

One of the challenges for park employees living without cars in Yellowstone is transportation. Seasonal workers want to get out and see as much as they can during their off-time, but there are not many public transportation options. If they live in Canyon and want to see Old Faithful, it's a forty-mile hike. Hitchhiking is the solution, and in Yellowstone it is considered safer than anywhere else in the country.

Hitchhiking stories abound in Yellowstone. Hikers on the side of the road with their thumb out and a smile, needing a ride back to their car or tent or housing, are a common sight in the park. A group of friends described being picked up in Mammoth Hot Springs by a truck driver from Idaho Falls who was hauling a truckload of supplies to West Yellowstone, a trip he made several times a month. He dropped the hikers off in Madison Junction, where they soon found a family traveling by RV with extra space to Old Faithful. On the way back they met a caravan of Canadians and rode with the ice chest (and cold beer) in the bed of a pickup truck, but they were back at their dormitory in time for dinner.

Drivers in Yellowstone have described picking up skiers holding their snowboards, trying to get up to Cook City for a day of skiing, and rafting hitchhikers who had just finished a day trip down the river, ten miles from their car. The park concessionaire provides bus service within the park (the park service discourages hitchhiking), but people say that the buses don't always fit their schedule and that they "meet a lot of nice people when [they] can hitch a ride."

The spirit of neighborliness is pervasive in Yellowstone National Park. Everyone knows that they must rely on each other in a place where there are not many people, roads, or vehicles and weather changes can be dramatic. It is a place where, as long as it's not a wild animal, drivers can feel comfortable that it's okay to be kind and stop for hitchhikers.

Smiling Down a Ride: Lisa, Jane, and Candy, seasonal employees from Taiwan, put on their best smile for a ride from Old Faithful to Madison Junction in Yellowstone National Park.

"Yellowstone is a remarkable source of information for human well-being."

Dave Lovalvo

Designer and builder of deep-water exploration devices

Scanning the surface of Yellowstone Lake from a boat, Dave Lovalvo and his crew aren't looking for fish. He's hunting for bubbles, sometimes so tiny that they barely pop at the surface of the frigid water. These bubbles are hints of thermals far below, oozing volcanic material escaping from the molten hot interior of the earth into the lake lying in the middle of a huge caldera. When the right spot is located, a very smart robot tethered to the boat will be sent down to video the scene and record the temperature and the chemical and microbial makeup of the ooze.

The designer, builder, and operator of the deep-submergence robot making its way downward, Dave has spent twenty-eight years exploring, filming, and mapping the Yellowstone National Park water systems and now works in many other locations around the world. He has been an engineering consultant to Woods Hole Oceanographic Institution, where he was certified by the U.S. Navy to pilot the manned deep submersible *Alvin* and was a member of the original design team for *Jason*, as well as for Dr. Robert Ballard's exploration vehicle *Hercules*. He was part of the team that built and installed Hydrolab, one of the first underwater habitats for science, and he was one of the chief pilots on expeditions to film the RMS *Titanic* and to locate John F. Kennedy's *PT-109* in the Solomon Islands.

His love for exploration began in his youth with a wreck he discovered while diving near his hometown on Long Island, and it expanded into commercial diving and eventual training as a navy diver.

"The human body can't hold up in the extreme conditions underwater where we need to collect information, so it made sense for me to invent a sophisticated robot that can do the work for us." As a self-described collector of material for scientists to study, he has explored and documented some of the most exciting underwater thermal features in the world.

Today, Dave leads the Global Foundation for Ocean Exploration, a nonprofit organization committed to developing innovative exploration tools to understand, interpret, and protect the world's oceans. Created by this talented team of engineers, videographers, educators, geologists, and oceanographers, a new robot, completely run on fiber optics, will collect data from vast, almost unreachable locations and make it available to all.

"You will be able to see previously inaccessible parts of the ocean floor on your cell phone," says Dave.

Seeing Below the Surface: Dave works on a remote-operated vehicle of his design.

"Music is almost always about place for me."

Jett Hitt

Composer, Yellowstone outfitter and trail guide

Many people have been enchanted by the magic of Yellowstone and inspired to express their experience in art and photography, but few have heard its overwhelming majesty and replicated that sound by writing music. In Jett Hitt's concerto *Yellowstone for Violin and Orchestra*, the listener is invited into both the serene beauty of the place and its wildest, most treacherous spots—perhaps unreachable except via the notes of Jett's extraordinary composition.

Jett grew up in a family that valued music education as well as living on a ranch, opening him to rich sensory experiences in both his inner and outdoor life. As a child, he learned to wrangle and break horses and was captivated by the musical score of *Star Wars.* With deep roots in the Ozark Mountains, a phenomenal musical sensibility, and a long line of cowboys before him, Jett was full of creative possibilities but still not prepared for what he saw on his first visit to Yellowstone, where he stopped by chance on a cross-country trip. "Not all places speak to me musically, but none has ever spoken as definitively as Yellowstone." His first sight of Electric Peak was the inspiration that would eventually become "Yellowstone," the first movement of his concerto.

Before the piece could be realized, he finished college with degrees in music and German. In 2001 he completed the first movement as his dissertation and received a doctorate in music composition. Fate eventually brought him to Idaho State University to teach for a semester. There, only two and a half hours from Yellowstone, he was able to spend every weekend in the park, and the second and third movements of his concerto, "Dunraven" and "Hoodoos," were inspired.

His ultimate immersion in Yellowstone, seven days a week, has been as a hugely popular licensed outfitter, leading hundreds of deep backcountry tours on horseback. Clients describe Jett's eighty-mile journeys by horse through the Thorofare of Yellowstone as incomparable experiences.

In describing a view that inspired him, Jett says: "Riding from Mammoth, the old Howard Eaton Trail passes out of the Hoodoos and narrows. To the left is a sheer drop-off straight down for hundreds of feet to Golden Gate Canyon. At the summit, I turned around and couldn't breathe. To look out over the Hoodoos at Golden Gate Canyon, Mount Everts, and Bunsen Peak is to know God. Hopefully I have given the listener a small impression of a horseback ride up to the top of creation."

Listeners hope that Jett finds more time and space to compose music.

Inspired by Paradise: Jett is owner of Yellowstone Wilderness Outfitters and a composer of classical music.

"I want mud on my boots and wind in my hair! I want to live Yellowstone!"

Jeff Henry

Photographer, writer, fishing guide, winter keeper

It's a crisp, sunny, -30 Fahrenheit day in Yellowstone and time to remove the six feet of snow on top of the general store buildings near Old Faithful geyser. The snow has "set" like Styrofoam and is ready to be sawed up into giant blocks and pushed off to avoid roof cave-ins or a dangerous avalanche. (Snow blocks are also heavy—some as much as a thousand pounds.) For Jeff Henry, a lover of cold weather and energetic work, it's a great day. The extreme weather conditions and endless snowstorms in the park require a crew of snow cutters and shovelers who, in anticipation of the winter's work, put ladders up against buildings and stash tools around the park every fall when the ground is bare. Jeff's only concern is that winters are becoming warmer and the snow may give out before he's ready to give up his job. "It doesn't snow as much these days, and it comes later and melts off earlier," he says.

Winter in Yellowstone National Park is also Jeff's favorite time to take notes for his written chronicles of winter on Yellowstone's volcanic plateau and to photograph "ghost trees"—frost-encrusted trees near geothermal outlets—and animals like bison and coyotes that tough it out in extreme weather.

Jeff says that it has been his destiny to be in Yellowstone. His parents started bringing him there on family vacations when he was six months old and took many iconic family photos of Jeff next to Fishing Bridge, geysers, and hot springs. After college, he arrived in Yellowstone "with his last dime"; walked into the personnel office in Gardiner, Montana; and was hired on the spot as a fishing guide on Yellowstone Lake.

Each year in May, in commemoration of that momentous event, Jeff celebrates with friends and usually takes a hike, regardless of the weather. Some of his 250,000+ photographs have appeared in *National Geographic*, *Time* magazine, *Big Sky Journal*, and many other publications. He has also published a total of eight books on Yellowstone, including three on the winter season.

The summer months are writing season, Jeff says. "I make myself sit there with a view out to the Yellowstone River until the words get moving. Sometimes I don't see another person for a week. Winter is for outdoor work and socializing. I know all the tour guides and snow coach drivers."

After more than thirty-eight years in the park, Jeff's fascination with Yellowstone has not changed. "I'm still captivated by the place, the lake, the wildlife, and love to share my passion with others," he says.

Snowman: Jeff with a variety of tools in the Old Faithful toolshed used for sawing and removing snow from roofs.

"Yellowstone is my chosen classroom. This is a sacred place."

Ashea Mills

Teacher, writer, snow coach driver, tour guide

The air was crisp and pine-scented when Ashea stepped from the Greyhound bus that carried her to Yellowstone back in 1995. After seeing an ad describing 2,000 summer jobs available in the park, she spent a month whittling down her belongings to what she could carry and took a leap of faith that there might be something for her in a wilder country. She arrived without a plan and no sense that her natural place in the world was waiting for her.

The gift shop in Mammoth Hot Springs provided not only a job, but a library. When customers were few, she jumped into the many books for sale about the park, the environment, and the animals. Stories about forest fires rekindled memories of her father's jobs as a fire lookout and wildland firefighter, including work on Yellowstone's historic fires of 1988. Interaction with visitors from all over the world and their questions about forest fires in particular made her realize that she had knowledge, from both reading and experience, and that interpreting facts delighted her. "I discovered the creativity of story," she says. "That magical feeling of passing along information in a way that made other people as captivated as I felt."

She also spent weekends on fifty-mile mountain treks and discovering the dramatic vistas of the Absaroka ridges and canyons cleaving Yellowstone. She saw hawks, bears, and bighorn rams and encountered elk, moose, and bison. She heard owls hooting, nighthawks trilling, and wolves howling.

Driving snow coaches was a natural transition. She loved the physical challenge of driving a Bombardier-load of people through the park in winter when the air was so cold that any moisture crystallized immediately into prismatic sparkles and the snow-covered landscape looked like a bowl of whipped cream. In the summer months, as an interpretive guide, stepping on buses to describe the area to visitors required a mixture of knowledge, passion for the place, and storytelling skills. "The way we introduce wilderness to people is extremely important. They need to understand the wildness and realize their responsibility to help keep wild places in existence." She went on to become a guide leading weeklong tours throughout the Yellowstone ecosystem and published related articles in a local magazine.

"Yellowstone helped me to reinvent myself," she says. "One night, standing amid the hot springs in Mammoth, under the moon, I realized that the wind can't blow through me. I exist. I'm rooted in Yellowstone. My prayer for Yellowstone is that my gratitude for what its mountain sentinels teach me will echo in my daily doings. I will honor its history and its presence, appreciate its details, and teach them to others."

Grateful: Ashea stands in the Boiling River hot spring in Gardner River, Yellowstone National Park.

"My secret desire was to be a rock-and-roll guitar player."

Stephen Edward Cole

U.S. magistrate judge in Mammoth Hot Springs

Stephen "Steve" Cole was born in Powell, Wyoming, in the "old hospital" and died in Powell in the "new hospital" at age sixty-five after a long battle with insulin-dependent diabetes. In between, he spent thirty-one years with his wife and three children as a much-beloved and respected judge in Mammoth Hot Springs, Yellowstone National Park. His brother-in-law described him as not only the most interesting, but also the most interested person he ever knew. He was curious about everything and everyone and always had a great sense of humor and wit, as well as a genius for recalling facts.

Steve had a unique job in Yellowstone as a federal judge living in and overseeing a national park, and he was only the fourth magistrate in the park's hundred-year history. Serious crimes such as rape and murder were transferred to the U.S. district court in Cheyenne, so in addition to drunk-driving and drug-related cases, he presided over lesser but unusual crimes that could happen only in Yellowstone—such as geyser vandalism, elk horn collecting, poaching, and photographers pestering bison.

During his time on the bench, law enforcement rangers appreciated Judge Cole's lack of tolerance for repeat offenders and those who tried to steal park resources such as shed elk antlers. A *Los Angeles Times* article in 1995 portrayed him as being not only judge, but also secretary, clerk, court recorder, and bailiff in what was perhaps the smallest courtroom in the West. Most importantly, he was kind and fair and had a deep respect for Yellowstone National Park.

In that interview, Steve described his career in Yellowstone by saying: "I've always looked at my life as a stick that somebody kicked into a creek, and it ended up here—which is not a bad place to be. I'm the luckiest guy on the face of the earth."

In Memoriam: Judge Stephen Edward Cole, 1947–2012.

"Cooking was a gift I learned from my mother."

Loretta Ehnes

Backcountry chef, woodstove cooking expert

It is Italian night at the hunting camp and the tables are decorated with vinyl red-checked tablecloths and candles in wine bottles, ready to seat twenty hungry men. As the guests file in from their tents, Loretta might be serving up spaghetti, fresh vegetables, fried chicken, homemade breads and pies, and red wine; or she may be serving breakfast with bacon, sausage, French toast, eggs, and homemade caramel rolls prepared the night before; or even fresh-caught fish, sage grouse, roast turkey, or venison. It's all delicious and prepared single-handedly on a woodstove using the nearest river or spring maybe three hundred feet away. Loretta has cooked for outfitters and hunting parties in the remote outback area surrounding Yellowstone for thirty years.

"I've met all kinds of people," she says, "and most of them appreciate a good meal."

Growing up on a North Dakota farm, she was introduced to cooking as soon as she was tall enough to manage the woodstove. She learned the art of preparing multiple foods at the same time on the same stove when she and her mother traded days working in the field and kitchen. By the age of nine, she could butcher, gut, and fry two chickens for the noon meal for eight people—by herself!

Little did she know that her early days on the farm were the perfect training ground for a job that requires packing in food, supplies, stove, and tents on thirty-five horses and riding for a whole day and half the night to reach camp. Some camps, high up on the fringes of Yellowstone, require crossing the Continental Divide twice in the same direction. On arrival, a full-course meal has to be prepared, even if it's midnight. Despite disruptions by rodents, snarling grizzly bear sows, accidental fires, and the occasional surly hunter, she feels thankful for the skills she learned from her mother. "I was born into cooking because, growing up on a farm, everyone had to work."

Loretta has two rules for safe camp cooking: keep a clean kitchen and keep the animals away from the food by using a cache in the trees and a bear box (a locked box strong enough to keep a bear out). She is also an extraordinary problem solver. If she forgets the lasagna noodles, no problem; she'll whip them up, roll them out, and hang them to dry on orange baling twine!

Today, she has left the wilds of the outback for more permanent quarters in her small tearoom in Cody, Wyoming, where there's always fresh bread, a pot of tea, and stories around the table.

Cookie: Loretta prepared gourmet "grub" under challenging conditions for deep woods hunters for over twenty-five years.

"Yellowstone is a magic place."

Bob Kisthart

Backcountry ranger, historian

Visitors who encounter a sharp-looking frontiersman at Bent's Old Fort National Historic Site in southeastern Colorado are meeting not only a re-enactor of life in the Old West, but also an individual with an extensive knowledge of how to survive in the wildest parts of Yellowstone National Park.

Bob Kisthart dresses in 1830s western-style buckskins while portraying the character he has created in his winter seasonal job at Bent's Old Fort. Using early-nineteenth-century journals and letters written by men (or about men), he seeks to portray a "typical" man of that era, living and working the western life of hunting, tracking, and surviving in the outdoors with only the simple pleasures—and perhaps nothing more than a blanket between him and the ground at night.

Bob's experience over several years as a backcountry ranger in Yellowstone was perhaps the best training he could have had to instill in him a deep understanding of such a character. As a ranger, he ventured out on horseback in all kinds of weather from a backcountry station to maintain three remote cabins nestled in the woods and as much as ninety miles of trail. He remembers coming upon the carcass of an elk once with a wolf dining on one end and a bald eagle on the other, and he often heard an eerie sound coming off the lake—like a finger rubbing the rim of a wine glass—that the rangers call "the lady of the lake."

"Every day was different," he says. "And at night I was treated to spectacular sights like the northern lights."

His route to becoming a ranger in Yellowstone was the result of persistence—along with a bit of serendipity. After passing through the park in October 1973, he returned every summer, working his way through jobs like driving a delivery truck for the gift shops, to kitchen worker, to bellhop and bell captain in the Old Faithful Inn. Every weekend was dedicated to hiking, camping, and getting to know the park.

"The northeast corner is the prettiest," he says. "But the southeast corner is the wildest." His advice to visitors is to have a healthy fear of wild animals but to get off the trail and explore the woods. "Get away from people and listen to nature," he suggests.

At the same time, Bob says he met some of the best people in the world at Yellowstone, people with soul and largesse of spirit who know that it's an honor and a sacrifice to work in the park. He's always glad to be back—buckskins and all.

Backcountry Man: Bob in buckskins recreating the history of the West at Midway Geyser Basin, Yellowstone National Park, Wyoming.

"Yellowstone is better than ever these days. It's ecologically sound, with a commitment to maintaining wildness."

Bob Barbee

Former Yellowstone National Park superintendent

Bob Barbee has experienced many "firsts" during his long career in the National Park Service, starting out as a guide at Carlsbad Caverns, where he "spent a lot of time in caves." As a young seasonal ranger and fledgling photographer in Yosemite, he worked alongside the great western photographer Ansel Adams, whom Bob describes as "a smart guy who really understood young photographers. He let us print some of his photos and then he'd sign them."

Bob held the first ranger position established at Point Reyes National Seashore before moving on to Big Bend National Park in Texas, where he enjoyed the wildness of the place but yearned for a ski trail. A stint in graduate school intervened before he returned to Yosemite to apply his knowledge of natural resource management to one of the first natural fire programs. As is often the case with dramatic changes in public policy, Bob had to "take the heat" as part of the first effort to institute a natural burn program, considered by some to be heretical.

For Bob, who would go on to challenge racial segregation at Cape Lookout in the Outer Banks of North Carolina and to work and live on an active volcano on the island of Hawaii, excellence in administration in difficult situations became his reputation. Challenging popular opinion in favor of solutions that benefit wildlife and maintain the natural habitat became his legacy. "Every place I went, I inherited a controversy."

Little did he know when he arrived in Yellowstone in 1983 that he would be at the helm during the unprecedented fires of 1988, battling to save the entire park, its historic structures, and the lives of firefighters. It was the largest wildfire in the recorded history of all national parks, burning 36 percent of Yellowstone.

Today, the Park Service has embraced the notion that forest fires are key to the health of the Greater Yellowstone Ecosystem. Managers no longer routinely suppress naturally occurring fires to preserve park resources. Bob and his colleagues, with their "radical ideas," have successfully convinced planners that fire promotes habitat diversity and allows native plant communities to become established. Fire also rapidly returns nutrients to the soil and allows for the sprouting and regrowth of plants, shrubs, and trees—particularly the lodgepole pine.

Changing a hundred years of history requires conviction, and Bob, as usual, was in the right place at the right time.

Burn: Forest fire control has changed since Bob Barbee's term as superintendent of Yellowstone, to a policy of natural prescribed fire management.

"I am fortunate to have my dreams come true. Yellowstone made it happen."

Joanne MacCartney

Yellowstone National Park maintenance crew member

When Joanne was growing up in Newport, Rhode Island, next to the Atlantic Ocean, the possibility of falling in love with a western landscape and living next to the magnificent Roosevelt Arch, the northern entrance to Yellowstone, never entered her mind. On the East Coast she might have seen a whale or two, but these days she has elk, deer, and 2,000-pound bison on her doorstep.

She first visited Yellowstone in 1986 with her boyfriend, Doug, while on vacation. They departed for home on the East Coast during a fall blizzard in Yellowstone, both wondering how they could come back and work in this splendid place.

By 1993 they were back, and both had jobs in the Yellowstone National Park maintenance department. Even the fickle weather of Yellowstone has been a charm in Joanne's life. When a summer snowstorm swept through on July 3 that year, their wedding, which was to take place on Swan Lake Flats, was moved to Mammoth Hot Springs Chapel. They eventually bought their home in Gardiner, Montana, with its unique proximity to the park and a view of majestic Electric Peak. Bull elk and bison graze near the front door to the house on their unfenced property. "For safety's sake, I just let them know I'm here when I walk out the door."

Joanne continues to love the physical challenge of her job, which includes everything from being a crusher crew member at the hot mix plant to working as a painter's assistant, to managing every aspect of meal preparation in winter for the snow removal crew. As the cook for nine seasons for fifteen hungry workers, she single-handedly ordered the food and supplies, cooked, and cleaned up in spite of sleet storms, blizzards, and workdays that could be fifteen hours long.

During her downtime, Joanne enjoys being outdoors, hiking, and camping. On one memorable trip to Pelican Valley, a grizzly bear that was protecting her three cubs charged her and two other hikers, coming within ten feet of the group. Fortunately, a blast of bear spray deterred the sow.

Despite the rigors of outdoor life, Joanne has lost none of her enthusiasm for Yellowstone. She loves the land and her job maintaining the park, gathering wood for winter, communing with the large animals who roam freely near her home, the friendships formed in the community—even the weather!

As Joanne says, "Yellowstone's snow is the best and brightest in the world. Spring, summer, and fall are great, too."

Can Do: Joanne embraces the joys and challenges of working outdoors in the park.

"Hiking in Yellowstone is my passion. I'll never get tired of it."

Jim Horan

Hiker, explorer, book distributor

We don't usually think of a long-distance hiker as being a "people person," but this is Jim: friendly, enthusiastic, and convivial. Hiking, he says, creates unique relationships with people, unlike any other experience. A hike can be a leisurely stroll through beautiful vistas or a push to the limits of physical capacity, but it is always a pleasure. Whether alone or talking with friends along the trail, each adventure, even on the same familiar route, is a once-in-a-lifetime experience. Hiking in Yellowstone has been his greatest romance, though.

After college he worked in the park for a concessionaire for three summers and five winters and as a backcountry ranger for the Park Service for two summers. He knew he had found his perfect place. "People are fewer and hardier in the winter, and they really want to be in Yellowstone."

Before spending his first winter in Yellowstone, he would not have described himself as a great skier, but soon he was skiing to work, and on his days off he winter-camped. After those first few seasons his life was transformed, and he knew Yellowstone had everything he needed. But how is it financially possible to stay in a place where you know you belong? After learning to make beer and opening a home brew store in Bozeman—Hellroaring Home Brew—he eventually found a job as a wholesale book distributor for stores within Yellowstone National Park.

For hiking, Hellroaring Mountain is his favorite place. He's hiked certain trails over and over. He describes walking around the Geyser Basin as a new experience every time. "It's always fresh and new because of the geysers and animals—the grizzlies especially."

The Black Canyon Trail, which winds along the Yellowstone River for twenty-three miles, is one of the earliest trails open for hiking in the spring, and Jim is always one of its first hikers. Jim says that Yellowstone has captured his heart and he's never lost his fascination with the place. He's seen the benefits of the rebounded wolf population, and he's fascinated with the supervolcano.

You'll find him every weekend on a hiking trail, alone or with friends, and during the week he has the pleasure of driving through the park as he checks on the bookstores' stock. For a lover of hiking, Yellowstone offers everything—fantastic trails, spectacular views and landscapes, and the opportunity to see animals in a place of untamed beauty.

Intrepid: Jim near the Continental Divide Trail, which runs through Yellowstone National Park.

"There is a federal mandate to protect the park. Yellowstone is a sacred place."

Jim and Heidi Barrett

Environmentalists, artists

The bison depicted in one of Jim Barrett's paintings doesn't seem to mind being captured on canvas in Jim and Heidi's airy and bright art gallery in downtown Livingston. Perhaps he knows he is more than an image to these activists and environmentalists who have battled to protect land and animals that are vulnerable to the needs and wants of humans.

When Jim arrived in Montana in May of 1972 via Detroit, Michigan, after serving in Vietnam, he remembers himself as being a naïve person moving into wilderness, bringing his own ideas and being acutely aware of threats against the environment. He had decided to search out "the coolest place" he could find. Driving through the beauty and immensity of the Lamar Valley, he knew he would be building a log cabin somewhere in the vicinity of this wondrous place, using an axe given to him by a friend for just that purpose.

Cooke City—a town surrounded by wilderness—was a logical destination for Jim and Heidi, with their talents for tackling any job available. He became handyman, caretaker, logger, carpenter, and eventually deputy sheriff—the "Kojak" of Cooke City. Heidi, an art teacher from Nebraska, worked as a waitress. Jim acquired a degree in fine art from the University of Montana.

Throughout all, both were inspired by a sense of awe and respect for wilderness.

"When you're from Detroit, you see a mountain as something sacred. I knew I needed to participate in preserving this place. Things going on outside the park affect the inside. There is no real boundary," says Jim.

When a gold mining company arrived with plans to tap the rich mineral area around the park, Jim and Heidi's concerns for the environment were put to the test. Together they formed the Beartooth Alliance, a local grassroots movement that joined forces with the Greater Yellowstone Coalition to stop the proposed New World Mine project adjacent to Yellowstone National Park. They were successful, and in 1997 Jim and Heidi were recognized with the National Parks Conservation Association's Marjory Stoneman Douglas Award for citizen activism.

After immersing themselves for years in the studies of both art and the Yellowstone ecosystem, they continue to be attentive to the survival of the wild inhabitants of the region.

"We can't treat the world as if it is our garden. What happens outside the park affects the inside. The larger discussion about gold mines, wolves, and bison has brought important attention to how the park can survive."

American Gothic, Silver Gate: Heidi and Jim in front of their hand-built house.

"Yellowstone is the world."

Tom Murphy

World-renowned nature and wildlife photographer

"One of the defining aspects of winter is the absence of many things. Color is absent or at least subdued, much of the wildlife is absent, most natural sounds are muffled by snow, and there is less daylight. This simplification draws attention to the basics of survival, elemental forms and shapes, clarity, concentration, and a distillation of what is most important."

This is how Tom Murphy describes his favorite season in *Winter: The Spirit of Yellowstone,* one of his four books describing the seasons in Yellowstone, when the temperature can drop to -40 Fahrenheit and "all plants and animals must modify their lives or die according to their ancient lessons." On his many photographic journeys through the park in winter he travels by cross-country ski in order to see what life is really like for creatures that live there year-round.

Weather was a big part of Tom's life as a child growing up on a cattle ranch on the open prairie in South Dakota, where the weather has been compared to that of Siberia: hot in the summer and cold in the winter. His parents came to Yellowstone often, and Tom was raised with an appreciation for solitude and wilderness. He started his working life as a commercial truck driver, but the lure of capturing the beauty and wildness of Yellowstone drew him to photography. On his first camping experience in the Yellowstone backcountry, he never saw another person for a week and thought, This is the place for me.

For almost four decades, Tom has photographed and taught photography at Yellowstone and throughout the world. His photographs have been used in numerous regional, national, and international publications.

In his early years of teaching, students requested areas where they wanted to go, but today he takes them wherever he chooses. He has experienced all areas of Yellowstone in all seasons, and his mission is to open people's eyes to what they can do to maintain the variety and diversity of the park while learning to photograph. He says that his celebrity status as a wildlife photographer has not always been comfortable, but it has given him the opportunity to make his own unique contribution to the park.

"I want them to learn to respect what's special about this place. I believe that people can learn to see in the quiet solitude of wildness."

Drawn to the Light: Tom Murphy has been photographing the beauty of Yellowstone in all seasons for more than four decades.

"Working in Yellowstone is not a dress rehearsal. It is an intense, real-life experience and it stays that way, day after day."

Suzanne Lewis

Former Yellowstone National Park superintendent

When she retired in 2011, after nine years as superintendent of Yellowstone and thirty-four years in the Park Service, Suzanne Lewis had not only managed 2.2 million acres and a staff of eight hundred in peak season, with an annual budget of $36 million (the largest of any national park); she was also the first woman ever to have been its top administrator. She described her final day: "Incredible! My last day in that special uniform I was so proud to wear."

Suzanne has a great empathy for the public who visit Yellowstone. "It takes a different set of skills," she says. "You can't approach it in the same way that you visit other places. People get a big bang for their buck. A drive down through the park presents a different challenge than any other road—a bear jam is something very different from a traffic jam on I-95."

"Nothing gave me more pleasure than speaking with visitors," she said. "Most people are in awe because they grew up seeing wild animals only in a zoo setting made to look like a natural habitat. At Yellowstone, where wild animals are not constrained in any way, it's another world."

Her advice to visitors is to be ready for an experience that is very different from home, and, while animals are free to roam, it doesn't mean that they are tame and approachable. Stay back! At least a hundred yards from wolves and bears and twenty-five yards from bison. You can be trampled, gored, or eaten.

During her years as its leader, she worked hard to ensure the park's survival.

"Everything in Yellowstone has the potential to be controversial. Wolves, bison, snowmobiles. I lead for the long term, not the short term."

But her lasting memory is of the dedicated people who work in Yellowstone, from painters who painstakingly work to restore antique structures, to those who clear trails in the backcountry, to those who translate the massive amounts of scientific information generated by research into consumable information in *Yellowstone Science* magazine.

She chose staff based on their passion for what they do. "When you find your passion, you find an ease of working. It isn't work anymore. Passion represents sincerity and genuineness. It takes special people to get their arms around such a great American treasure. It's an intense, unforgettable life experience to work here."

Proud: Suzanne stands in front of the officers' quarters in Mammoth Hot Springs on the day of her retirement as superintendent of Yellowstone National Park.

"Heavy Lifting"

David Todd

Construction crane operator

Seismic activity in Yellowstone is exciting to observe when it appears on the surface of the earth—the park sits atop a massive underground volcano—but for those who construct buildings, roadways, and bridges, everything must be built according to specific guidelines in order to prevent damage from earthquakes.

David Todd witnessed the natural wonders of the park from a close-up perspective when he worked on the $7.5 million project to replace the decaying seventy-five-year-old year-old Lamar River bridge. The new bridge is a three-span, 420-foot-long, haunched steel plate girder, a design that allows the use of lighter beams over a longer area and built to withstand the high seismic activity and active faults within fifty miles of the bridge. An additional challenge for designers was to match the existing structures in the park while still blending in with the natural environment.

Besides the physical challenges of bridge-building and managing massive heavy equipment during the two-year project, David witnessed both traffic jams involving cars and also migrating animals moving from their winter grazing lands to their southern habitat each year. Perched in his crane, it was a daily treat to observe bison, wolves, grizzlies, elk, and many other animal species.

Not only was he working in one of the most beautiful areas of Yellowstone amid abundant wildlife, but the bridge itself was selected as one of the winners of the 2014 International Bridge Conference Photographic Contest—Bridges of the U.S. Federal Lands.

What could be better than to be surrounded by both natural and human-made beauty in the area known as the Serengeti of Yellowstone National Park.

New Bridge: Dave on the job as crane operator for the construction of the new Lamar River Bridge.

"There is a long history of excellent service to guests at the Old Faithful Inn. I had a lot to live up to."

John Salvato

Bell captain at the Old Faithful Inn and Snow Lodge, snow coach driver

When the Old Faithful Inn opened in the spring of 1904, it boasted of not only electric lights and steam heat, but also a well-trained staff ready to provide extraordinary service to weary guests arriving by wagon, stagecoach, and horseback.

Before visitors disembarked to enter the spectacular lobby built of logs and tree limbs and to view the massive five-hundred-ton, eighty-five-foot stone fireplace, they were surrounded by staff, led by the bell captain, ready to carry their bags up to their rooms and assist them with their needs. It was the golden age of architecture and guest services.

John Salvato, who arrived in 1990 after escaping "a nowhere job back in New York," felt lucky to work his way up to the coveted job of bell captain at the magnificent and renowned Old Faithful Inn, where he maintained its reputation for fine service.

"It was a privilege to work in my position, and I know people don't get to experience very often the kind of service we provide. We make the first impression, and our goal is for each guest to feel welcome and relaxed."

John supervised two greeters and seven bell staff. Carrying masses of luggage down to the lobby on narrow staircases in the early morning and then carrying more back up to rooms as the next flock of guests arrived provided great training for hiking and mountaineering. Another benefit of being on the bell staff was the opportunity to live high up on top of the inn in "Bat's Alley," which opens out onto the roof and "Pebble Beach" (stones cemented to the roof): a magnificent spot for viewing meteor showers and the northern lights. Being bell captain of a historic hotel also meant having many unique responsibilities. In his earlier years at the Old Faithful Inn, John wound the giant antique clock when it was in service. Throughout the years, he also raised and lowered the American and state flags that fly high above the inn. This meant climbing eighty-six steps and gaining sixty feet in elevation above the lobby floor. "The first couple of times I was scared to death of the height and nervous. I never took it lightly."

As a snow coach driver for ten years, he experienced one of the highlights of his park career when he transported the 2002 Olympic flame from West Yellowstone, Montana, to a ceremonial lighting at Old Faithful.

"Yellowstone changed my life completely."

With Honor: John folding the American flag that flies from the top of Old Faithful Inn.

"I'll never forget the view of that stunning park from atop my horse, Big Red. We covered twenty to twenty-five miles a day."

Bob Richard

Yellowstone National Park ranger (retired), guide, author

The Richard family knows the Yellowstone region, with a tradition stretching back to a time before Yellowstone was even established as the park it is today. From his ranch in Cody, Wyoming, Bob reflects back on a career that started as a seasonal ranger on a beloved horse named Big Red during his college years, and a relationship with the place that started long before.

"It's hard for me to put into words all the feelings I have toward Big Red and that early time in Yellowstone. I shared the beauty of the outdoors with the best horse I've ever known when I patrolled Yellowstone from 1956 to 1960."

He was introduced to Yellowstone at age six by his grandfather, who had toured the park during the early part of the twentieth century when it was still under the control of the U.S. Cavalry. In those days, his grandfather visited Yellowstone during a sixteen-day tour on horseback and wagon—and that's how he met Bob's grandmother.

As a ranger carrying out his duties in the late 1950s, Bob also met his wife in Yellowstone when he asked her to stop feeding the bears. In 1960, upon graduation from college, he received a commission in the U.S. Marine Corps and went on to fly fifty combat missions during the Vietnam War. Eventually, family ties brought him back to a ranch in Cody and he reconnected with his beloved Yellowstone, working as a guide conducting family and bus tours. His youngest son now carries on the family tradition as a park guide.

Bob has published three books about the park and the surrounding areas and has traveled throughout Yellowstone on horseback. He says, "I love sharing my backyard with people, and my favorite place is the Lamar Valley." His next book will be about five generations of Yellowstone guiding.

Bob's favorite memory is of the personality and demeanor of Big Red, the last Morgan horse at Yellowstone, the end of a bloodline that had been brought into the park to improve the stock back in 1940.

"In those years at Yellowstone, that reliable Morgan sorrel never let me down a single day we were together. Big Red took care of me, never spooked or faltered, was always with me on the trails.... He was the perfect representative of the most famous national park in America: stunning, strong, and true."

Family Tradition: Bob's father, a photographer, captured many photos of the Richard family's life in Yellowstone over the years.

"More big animals are killed in Yellowstone by vehicles on roadways than any other cause. For the sake of elk, bison, deer, and others, please, slow down!"

Beth Kreuzer

Backcountry ranger, wildlife advocate, citizen scientist

In 1990, Beth Kreuzer was killing time reading *Country Life* magazine during a break from her job as a homicide detective in the Houston (Texas) police department when she happened on an article about an organization led by Dr. Bob Crabtree, founder of Yellowstone Ecosystem Studies. The article invited readers to become citizen scientists by spending twelve days working in the wild with one of the most feared and endangered mammals: the grizzly.

Beth couldn't resist. With her desire to challenge herself both physically and mentally, she jumped at the chance. After her first immersion into the real world of wild animals, she became convinced that humans were the root cause of dwindling wildlife populations. She returned summer after summer, volunteering as a camp cook and getting a close look at animal research in the wild. Eventually, this experience led to a volunteer position as a grizzly researcher working with Lance Craighead and the Craighead Environmental Research Institute, focusing on how people could save, rather than decimate, the species of wildlife that were present when the park first opened in 1872. Her current rugged job of backcountry ranger was a natural transition.

"I've looked at hundreds of human murder victims in my police work, and I'm just as affected when I see a buffalo or an elk slaughtered on a roadway. More than a hundred big mammals are killed every year by people driving too fast in the park."

As a ranger, she checks trails on horseback, rescues campers, issues permits, and gives instruction to hundreds of backpackers on the art of keeping food away from hungry bears. At just over five feet tall, her petite size has never been an impediment; wielding an axe, dealing with large dead animals, and clearing fallen trees from trails are all part of the job.

She describes herself as a "travel agent" in her ranger job, answering a multitude of questions from visitors about where to go and what to do in the park for the best experience. But she can also be described as an unrelenting protector of Yellowstone and its natural inhabitants.

"As a ranger, I do a multitude of things, but my most important job is reminding people to act responsibly toward each other and the wild animals who live here."

Crimes against Nature: Beth contemplates the bison skull, which is used in ranger presentations and was moved for this portrait to Fountain Flats, Yellowstone National Park.

"This is the land of my dreams."

Robert G. Whipple

Yellowstone National Park ranger, sport plane pilot, engineer, master builder

Ranger Bob Whipple's earliest connection with the West was a bag of smooth river stones brought back from Montana to Connecticut by his great-grandmother when she traveled by Model-T Ford through what was then a rough and wild terrain in the 1920s. She also brought back stories of bears being hand-fed by people and streams bursting with trout.

"As a child growing up on the East Coast, we didn't hear so much about the West except for Roy Rogers and Gene Autry on TV, but my great-grandmother brought it to life with her descriptions of wild animals and magnificent forests."

In 1971, he graduated from college with dual degrees in engineering and business administration and decided to take a road trip across the country to see some of that wildness he'd heard about. He was not disappointed. When he arrived in Yellowstone and stood on Fishing Bridge, he looked down into the river at hundreds of cutthroat trout, glimmering like rubies, preparing to spawn. "The river was thick with trout in those days, and the place seemed like paradise."

He went on to Cornell University to complete a master's degree in health administration. Juggling house-building projects that involved complex engineering and duties as a partner and builder in the family nursing home business, he continued to work on the East Coast while dreaming of the West. He returned summer after summer to volunteer in Yellowstone and purchased land to build the ultimate house, an architectural wonder in a spectacular location: Big Sky. His design of steel and glass grips the mountainside and suits the character of this easterner with a love for the West.

Today he works in Yellowstone during the summer season as an interpretive ranger, providing programs for visitors about everything from bears to owls to forest fires, and continues to challenge himself with engineering innovations to his mountaintop home. He thinks Yellowstone is the best place in the world: "I want visitors to have an emotional connection with the park—like me. Yellowstone today is more than it was ever imagined to be in the past."

He's thankful for his explorer ancestors who brought back mementos that inspired him to discover the wonders of the West, but in his fireside talks and encounters with visitors to Yellowstone, he reminds people to leave the stones where they are rather than take them home as souvenirs. "Leave it here for others to enjoy," he says.

Proud to Serve: Bob, standing in front of his mountain home, is honored to wear the uniform of the National Park Service.

"When I found this job, I knew it was made for me in heaven."

Reverend Doctor William "Bill" Young

Former resident minister, Mammoth Hot Springs, Yellowstone National Park

For Bill Young, one of only three ministers who serve the spiritual needs of people in the country's national park system, it wasn't essential to come together with his congregation in traditional places. Church existed wherever residents in Mammoth could gather and speak about their lives, including trout streams, hiking trails, camping spots, and barn-raising projects.

Being a compassionate listener and spiritual problem solver while fishing and camping comes naturally for Yellowstone's resident minister, who grew up hunting and fishing in West Virginia. Since 1983 he has served as pastor of both the chapel in Mammoth and Gardiner Community Church outside of the park. The U.S. government does not financially support any religious organizations within the park. The church and its members raise all support.

Reverend Young says that, besides its natural beauty, Yellowstone inspires metaphors that can help guide people's lives. Noting the predictability of Old Faithful, he is attentive to the message it imparts that he can pass along to his parishioners. And then there was the time that the gorgeous deep blue and orange colors of the Morning Glory Pool that ascend from deep within the earth through underwater vents were dimmed because the vents were blocked by objects thrown in by people. This image, he said, provided the perfect segue for a lesson about how we deal with the burdens in our lives. Daily ministerial issues and duties in a national park community sound somewhat similar to life almost anywhere: marriages, births, deaths, spousal abuse, substance abuse, grief counseling, marital problems, and—these days—destination weddings. He recently married a couple from Ireland who wanted to be married only in Yellowstone. Mammoth has a cemetery, but no one has been buried there for years.

As one of its ministries, the church took a youth group to Mexico to build houses in a poor area. "It was a culture shock for the kids," he says. "They all learned a lot."

"I'm constantly reminded that I work in a crown jewel of God's kingdom, and Mammoth is a wonderful place for children to grow up. We don't need to lock our doors and people take care of each other. It's hard to come to a place like Yellowstone and not be confronted by spiritual questions in the midst of all this majesty. I'm honored to have been able to come here to listen and be their guide."

Spiritual Guidance: Reverend Young in Mammoth Chapel, Mammoth Hot Springs, Yellowstone National Park.

"There's a lot to learn in Yellowstone."

Charissa Reid

Writer, editor, historian, science interpreter, lifelong member of the Yellowstone community

Visitors on the boardwalk path that passes a bubbling hot spring in Mammoth are amazed by the powerful plumes of water and steam gushing up from the earth and mesmerized by the transparent blue pools of boiling water. What they may not realize is that the minerals in these same hot springs have provided scientists with information about subjects as diverse as kidney stone formation in humans and how coral reefs in the Caribbean change.

As a contributor and graphic designer for *Yellowstone Science* magazine, Charissa's goal is to make the vast amount of scientific research that occurs continuously in Yellowstone available and accessible not only to scientists, but to everyone who wants to learn more about Yellowstone. "This is a beautiful place," she says, "but there's also a lot to learn here. My job is to translate science into something that people can understand."

She is uniquely qualified to appreciate Yellowstone's subtle and wondrous qualities. Growing up in Mammoth, where her father was the resident minister, she recalls his advice to his children and to parishioners: "If you're bored in Yellowstone, you're just not paying attention." Charissa and her husband, Tim, have enjoyed raising their three daughters in her childhood home.

At age eighteen, Charissa began her lifelong career in the National Park Service. After a stint as a fee collector and dispatcher in Rocky Mountain National Park, she worked in Yosemite, Joshua Tree, Death Valley, Pinnacles, Grand Canyon, and Badlands National Park before returning to Yellowstone as an interpretive ranger in 1994. Her book, *Expedition Guide to Yellowstone,* demonstrates her deep understanding of the park and how to enjoy it, and won the National Outdoor Book Award.

"A lot is behind the scenes here and has to be explored to be discovered. Most visitors don't venture far enough out to find things. Only about 5 percent of people attend programs with interpretive rangers. The Junior Ranger program is a great way for kids to get involved, and everyone should take at least one hike!"

She suggests a three-day minimum itinerary: a "hot water" day visiting the Mars-like Mammoth terraces, the very acidic Norris Geyser Basin, and the Midway geyser; a "cold water" day up to Tower Falls and Upper and Lower Falls; and a "wildlife" day in the Lamar Valley, called the Serengeti of America, getting up early to see birdlife and wolves. She urges people to stay long enough to see and enjoy as much as possible. She's been in Yellowstone her entire life and is still astounded by the place.

Awestruck: Charissa with members of her family on land purchased by her parents in the 1970s in Gardiner, Montana.

"I'm endlessly curious about the earth, especially earthquakes, and Yellowstone provides lots of information."

Robert "Bob" Smith

Seismologist, geologist, researcher, teacher

Some people might be disturbed if the earth began to move beneath their feet, but for Dr. Robert Smith it was love at first sight—or first quiver.

Bob was born in northern Utah and grew up in Jackson Hole, Wyoming. He doesn't remember a single visit as a child to Yellowstone. For him, serendipity and a keen sense of observation would lead to his career in seismology and an intimate knowledge of earthquake activity in the Yellowstone region.

Bored with high school in 1956, he quit to take a job with the U.S. Fish and Wildlife Service. His observations of aspects of Yellowstone lake launched a fascination with the surfaces of dry land and lake bottoms. He noticed things that others did not necessarily observe, or care about, at the time. Back in the fifties, little note had been made of the science behind rock formations and changes within the earth. Bob noticed "bathtub rings" around lakes and land basins, the reciprocity between a surface in one area and another surface far away. He began to seek answers in situations where even the questions had not been formulated. His supervisor at the time reminded him that he was supposed to be interested in the fish rather than the lake. But Bob had other fish to fry. He researched old elevation studies made in 1923 and noted that, twenty-five years later, the ground was now two feet higher. Was it an error of measurement? The quest to figure out why this dramatic change had occurred in so few years captured his imagination, and, fifty-eight years later, he is still observing the geological wonders of Yellowstone.

Today, ultrasensitive instruments and sophisticated technology can be used to measure an earthquake of any magnitude even in the quietest range. Now, he says, it's possible to look under the earth and have a 3-D view—similar to having an MRI scan of the earth. Up to 2,000 earthquakes are now detected and recorded each year. Yellowstone is the most seismically active area in all of the Rocky Mountains.

The last big volcanic eruption, the Yellowstone Caldera, occurred 650,000 years ago, leading to speculation that another event is imminent. But Bob says: "Relax. Yellowstone is dynamic and active, but we probably have a few thousand years before the next big one."

Bob has encouraged his PhD students to seek out their own questions. "Stay curious. Curiosity is your friend when it comes to understanding this wondrous planet."

Super Volcano Man: Bob at the columnar basalt formations of Sheepeater Cliff in Yellowstone National Park.

"Yellowstone's biggest environmental challenge will be educating the millions of annual visitors in only a day and a half—the average stay for most tourists—on understanding environmental stewardship."

Jim Evanoff

Environmental protection specialist

When most people think of Yellowstone they envision geysers, wild animals, and spectacular scenery—not trash. But the millions of visitors each year generate about 4,000 tons of garbage. Jim Evanoff believes that national parks are the perfect laboratory for introducing efficient and effective recycling programs that promote a greener environment. He honed his skills while working in four other national parks, developing infrastructure and preserving historic sites—including one job that allowed him to rappel off the top of Mount Rushmore to clean the famous four faces—before moving on to Yellowstone, where for twenty-four years he has identified and overseen many of the park's sustainability initiatives and environmental programs. Dealing with 4,000 tons of trash each year has posed his ultimate creative challenge. Jim takes a logical approach and asks: Where does it come from, where does it go, and how can it be reused?

Following the trail of forty-five tons of plastic generated annually—mostly water bottles—Jim discovered that the plastic was sold and transported first to a broker in Montana; from there it went to Seattle and finally got sent overseas, where the plastic disappeared. His solution was to recycle and reuse. Now, the plastic waste goes to a Georgia company that recycles it into carpet backing that returns to Yellowstone to be installed in park hotels and other applications around the country. Similarly, glass bottles are crushed in Livingston and used in a variety of applications throughout the tristate region. Organic waste is composted at a facility outside of West Yellowstone and then used in landscaping projects. Jim's creative stewardship initiatives in recycling and reuse are evident throughout Yellowstone and have spread to national parks throughout the country. He is quick to give credit to visitors, though. "More and more people are visiting our national parks and expecting them to be well-managed."

On the eve of Jim's retirement from the park, Karen Kress, president of the Yellowstone Foundation (now Yellowstone Forever), described her perplexity at how anyone could replace Jim. "He was Mr. Sustainability," she said.

"If I miss my job, I'll do something about it. Until then, I've got a few ideas. There's nothing like standing along the Old Faithful boardwalk on a summer day as people gather to watch their geyser," said Jim.

Sustainable: Jim stands in front of a generator instrument panel, formerly used in Yellowstone National Park, powered by the energy of falling water through domestic water piping to supplement electricity production for the local utility company.

"Education is important for visitors because bears can be dangerous."

Jeff Brown

Director of Yellowstone Association, survivor, educator

Stepping into the elegant glass entryway of the Yellowstone Association (now Yellowstone Forever) in Gardiner, Montana, near the Roosevelt Arch, it's obvious that this is a place dedicated to educating visitors about all that the park has to offer. Since 1933, the Yellowstone Association has been a nonprofit partner of Yellowstone National Park, reaching out to people of all ages; providing over six hundred courses and programs for teachers and the general public; and maintaining a research library, field campuses in the Lamar Valley and Gardiner, and much more. Its membership program is 40,000 strong and supportive of the breadth and variety of offerings, from wolf discovery to Yellowstone on skis.

At the helm is Jeff Brown, an educator with a range of backcountry experience that is surpassed by few. More than twenty years ago, Jeff survived a life-threatening bear mauling which left him with sixty-six surgical wounds after being dragged more than 189 feet and bitten and scraped by an angry grizzly.

"The most frightening part," said Jeff, "was this large male bear straddling me, flipping me over with his paw and panting into my face."

Jeff and a friend had hiked about seven miles into what they knew was bear country near Granite Park Chalet in Glacier National Park. They heard a growl, and suddenly a bear was charging within fifty yards. Both had been rangers, so they stood their ground, waved their arms, and tried to deter the charge. At the last moment his friend tried to climb a tree; the bear first attacked her and then focused on Jeff. His friend escaped and ran for help, even with a muscle torn from her calf.

Jeff's courage and determination have allowed him to continue hiking and exploring the backcountry. On the twenty-fifth anniversary of the event he went back and hiked the same trail. He believes that, besides the luck of finding help, they were saved by the knowledge they had about what to do in the midst of a surprise attack.

"Bears are big, powerful animals and are not to be fooled with. Armed with the right information and knowledge, and taking reasonable precautions, people can share the outdoors with them."

Jeff also says that wild places are calming, and he considers himself fortunate to live and work at the base of mountains in a beautiful environment. "The more I've learned and experienced, the more I love this place that is Yellowstone."

Inspiring: Jeff holds the shirt he was wearing when he was mauled by a bear in Glacier National Park.

"I'm so fortunate to work in a beautiful place and preserve its cultural history."

Bridgette Guild

Museum registrar, curator

Most of us are surrounded by random objects that reflect who we are; where we've been; the hobbies we've enjoyed and hope to resume; the books, souvenirs, and photographs that accumulate over the years.

But imagine that you are the collector and organizer of objects that describe the story of a place—like Yellowstone or the Grand Tetons—or the establishment of statehood for Idaho, Wyoming, or Montana. As a curator and museum registrar, working carefully with white cloth gloves, Bridgette Guild has cataloged the original nineteenth-century letter from President Teddy Roosevelt concerning the issue of grazing land for ranchers in the area of Yellowstone.

When producers for Ken Burns' television series on the national parks needed old photographs and historic material, she was able to dip into the archives and find not only innumerable photographs, but also items from the 1800s, including a letter written by Daniel Potts in the 1820s about his visit to the Yellowstone area. Among other treasures are the 1871 Thomas Moran watercolor paintings depicting western landscapes with thermal features that were far more convincing to Congress than any oral descriptions and helped to persuade President Grant that the area should be preserved.

Besides receiving donations of items and assessing their relevance to the historical culture of the area, Bridgette responds to many requests by historians, scientists, and other researchers to provide scanned materials for study, including a cataloged collection of microbes!

"Yellowstone is a great example of how scientific research has changed. With its vast collections, the staff is able to provide access to study material for researchers all over the world, from European scientists doing geology work, to New Zealanders and Japanese scientists looking at changes in plant species. The result is many different spins on the same subject of research."

The Yellowstone National Park Service and museum staff members are continually concerned with how science and people interact. Besides scientific discoveries relevant to medical research, climate change, and other issues, the knowledge accumulated through observation, collection, and cataloging has even been utilized to create apps that guide visitors so they can maximize their enjoyment of all that Yellowstone has to offer.

"The park doesn't change—but we are understanding more and more of what it is," says Bridgette.

Preserve: Bridgette with some of the many artifacts and specimens that are collected and stored for the Heritage and Research Center Museum in Gardiner, Montana. She is currently curator at Grand Teton National Park Museum.

"When you see a waterfall, the memory sticks with you."

Mike Stevens

Waterfall discoverer, Yellowstone tour guide, author

Mike Stevens' unique relationship with Yellowstone all started years ago with a personal challenge: visit all the known waterfalls in Yellowstone (about 50 at that time in 1996) and perhaps find a few that are not yet indicated on park maps. Mike and fellow waterfall stalkers Lee Whittlesey and Paul Rubinstein have since documented more than 225 Yellowstone waterfalls never before mapped, named, photographed, or described. Along the trail they met grizzlies, had close calls with lightning strikes, and discovered a remote area with so many waterfalls that they named it "Valhalla." Their pursuit of waterfalls is described in *The Guide to Yellowstone Waterfalls and Their Discovery*.

But Mike has also become a legend in his own right. He will soon celebrate thirty-five years as a Yellowstone summer employee and twenty years as a step-on bus tour guide. He provides lectures and guided tours, and the word is out that he is your man if you would like to visit remote waterfalls and see spectacular views that few others, if any, have seen. He has hiked thousands of miles in pursuit of previously unseen and unmapped trickling or gushing water that falls from a height of at least fifteen feet and is an impediment to fish (the definition of a waterfall).

His reputation for his discoveries has spread beyond the park, and he is proud to have been credited in several books about Yellowstone, including an atlas of the park created by the University of Oregon. While guiding a *National Geographic* team to view waterfalls, it was a thrilling moment when he reminded them that they were "only the fourth or fifth pair of eyes to see this."

Mike's desire to share his enthusiasm for what he loves was evident back in the 1980s when he formed a club to take his high school students to Yosemite National Park for an annual trip to see waterfalls. He had found his passion and has never tired of it. His personal favorite is a waterfall in Yellowstone that has a dry watershed. After following a dry creek bed for a quarter of a mile, he discovered a waterfall that simply soaked into the earth and disappeared rather than creating a stream. The "Surprise Falls" would later become the site of his wedding to another park employee whom he had introduced to waterfall hunting.

Are there still more waterfalls to find in Yellowstone? Mike is optimistic: "As long as I can hike, I'll keep looking."

Wonderland of Waterfalls: Mike spent more than seven years finding and documenting unknown waterfalls in Yellowstone National Park.

"Yellowstone is such a big melting pot for people from all over. It blew my horizons wide open."

Bill Berg

Founder of CoolWorks.com, an online job board for "jobs in great places"

Bill Berg is all about making connections between people and the right job. "Yellowstone was a breakaway from my Lake Wobegon childhood," he said. He first visited as a nineteen-year-old college student for a summer job in Yellowstone as a gas station attendant.

After college, he patched together summers managing Yellowstone gas stations, working for the National Outdoor Leadership School, and working as a backcountry ranger in Alaska and Yellowstone, all while working as a "winter keeper" at Old Faithful, then Lake station, protecting the buildings from heavy snow loads. Eventually he became director of operations for Yellowstone Park Service Stations (YPSS), which is where his talent for connecting job seekers with potentially life-changing seasonal work emerged. He also managed some superb matchmaking for himself when he met and married Colette Daigle-Berg, a Yellowstone National Park ranger who also got her start as a gas station attendant.

One of his tasks with YPSS was to hire summer staff for the park each year. When he started an MBA program in environmental management in 1995, he made another important discovery: the Internet.

Internet connectivity was still new in 1995, and the largest group with access was college students with free access via their student accounts. "Millions of college students had free Internet access and free summers—and I knew employers with thousands of summer jobs to fill. The web seemed like the perfect tool for connecting the two," said Bill. And so CoolWorks, a web-based job matching service, was born at Tower Junction in Yellowstone. Employers pay CoolWorks to list their work opportunities for wait staff, room cleaners, river guides, bellhops, ski operators, and more, and the website connects them with American and international college students and job seekers of all ages looking for a way to live and work where others vacation.

The object in Bill's hand in the photo is a pen with floating stars that Bill considers his "magic wand." When hiring people to work in Yellowstone, he feels he is offering a job that could change their life and he gives them the CoolWorks traditional blessing: a wave with his pen. What could be better than finding the perfect job for the perfect person in this sacred place? It's a match made in heaven.

Matchmaker: Outside the "web shack" in Gardiner, Montana, Bill is in the shadow of the satellite dish that connects CoolWorks to the world.

"Yellowstone, like any of the national parks, is a gift we give ourselves."

Michael Finley

Formerly Turner Foundation president and Yellowstone National Park superintendent

When Ted Turner learned that his longtime fishing and hunting partner Mike Finley was retiring after thirty-two years with the national park system in 2001, he offered him the perfect job as president and treasurer of the Turner Foundation. This position would draw on Mike's unique experiences crossing the U.S. six times while working as superintendent of Yosemite National Park and for the Everglades National Park, Assateague Island National Seashore, and many other parks. As superintendent of Yellowstone, his legacy included the reintroduction of wolves to the park.

Back in his college days at Southern Oregon University, Mike was attracted to a career in dentistry, but he also enjoyed seasonal jobs working in fire control at Yellowstone. While mulling over his future with a practicing dentist, he was advised to follow his heart—which had always led him to working outside on the land.

The rest is more than history. Mike pursued ranger positions from Alaska to Texas. He directly managed hunting and fishing activities on National Park Service lands and waters in Alaska, Florida, Maryland, Virginia, California, Montana, and Wyoming. He is a commissioned law enforcement ranger, was an investigator for ten years, and has been responsible for legislative affairs in Washington, D.C.

Mike is a legend as an advocate for the national park system, insisting that resources always come first and that fidelity to the law in park administration is crucial to survival. While working as a park ranger, he enjoyed meeting visitors who would ask: "What should we do today?" He knew that no matter what they chose to do, they would have a fabulous day, because Yellowstone is such a spectacular place.

How does he decide when to move on to the next adventure? Mike says he thinks of the efforts required to help a natural environment survive as a kind of "music." He says, "Keep listening to the music and stay until the noise is louder than the music."

In his role at the Turner Foundation, he worked toward conserving both public and private land, establishing marine protected areas, and restoring endangered species. He also facilitated sustainable practices in partnership with trade organizations such as the National Restaurant Association and the American Hotel and Lodging Association. There is no doubt that he would have been an excellent dentist, but thankfully he chose the land.

The Face of Conservation: Michael continues to support environmental causes around the world.

"I call myself a modern-day gypsy, living as close to nature as I can."

MerryCline Pickenpaugh

Seasonal park employee, hiker, disc golfer

MerryCline didn't bat an eyelash at seeing forty-five rattlesnakes and twenty-five copperhead snakes during her six months of hiking from Georgia to Maine on the Appalachian Trail in 2013. She was well trained and conditioned thanks to seven years in Yellowstone, where she had hiked more than a thousand miles. Her seasonal jobs—working in the Old Faithful Inn gift shop and Native American gallery, waitressing in the dining room, and guiding visitors on snow coaches—offered plenty of opportunity for her to enjoy sports activities with other workers and head deep into backcountry trails for hiking and camping.

The Old Faithful Wilderness Course version of disc golf was a highlight. Having been a tournament winner and a player in Las Vegas, Virginia, North Carolina, Montana, Wyoming, and Idaho helped prepare her for Yellowstone's unique twist on the sport. Instead of shooting the ball at traditional baskets, players shoot at natural objects like rocks, stumps, and logs. But watch out for animal strokes (hitting an animal; bears, elk, bison, foxes, wolves, and other creatures are common sights on the course), and avoid beer strokes (knocking over your own or someone else's beer). Each earns a one-stroke penalty!

MerryCline's first loves, though, are hiking and exploring the wilderness. She has reached the top of Eagle Peak, Yellowstone's tallest peak, and explored most of the remote trails, all while carrying everything on her back. "I've seen every animal in the park except a mountain lion."

One of her favorite trails is Bechler Meadows, which runs from Old Faithful all the way to the Bechler ranger station in Wyoming, just on the border of Idaho. "There are more than ten waterfalls … and a hot pool to soak in after long days of hiking."

Besides tales of her animal and hiking experiences, she also has gift shop stories. Among her favorites are two questions from visitors: "When does an elk turn into a moose?" and "At what elevation do antlers grow?" "I always suggest that they try to get out of their comfort zone—hit the trail and find a waterfall!"

Guests also ask: "When are you going back to the real world?" And MerryCline replies, "This is my real world. What's next is a new hiking adventure right outside my doorstep. Living and working in Yellowstone isn't meant for everyone, but it certainly is for me. I'll be back. Again and again."

Up, Up, and Away: MerryCline demonstrates disc golf in Yellowstone National Park.

"When I discovered Yellowstone and read about Lewis and Clark, I realized I had been born two hundred years too late!"

Norm Miller

Hiker, kayaker, educator, preservationist, time traveler

In Norm's earliest memory of Yellowstone, it is 1968. He was five years old and face-to-face with a four-hundred-pound black bear. As the bear's giant paw closed in, it snatched the jelly doughnut that Norm's sister had pushed through a four-inch opening in the window of the family station wagon. With a powdered-sugar nose, the bear loped away to the next car in line. This was not an unusual experience for visitors to the park until the National Park Service forbade the feeding of wildlife, both for the protection of visitors and to improve the diet of animals. But for Norm it was a life changer.

The Miller family came back, year after year, even if they couldn't feed the bears, and Norm was smitten with this wild country. Yellowstone evoked the Wild West and fueled his dreams of trailblazing.

Summer jobs waiting tables in park concessions left him feeling that he had been born two hundred years too late. John Colter of the Lewis and Clark expedition was beckoning him back to 1804 when a group of young men were enlisted to explore the vast territory acquired in the Louisiana Purchase.

So what if the expedition had started without him a few years back! Norm steeped himself in the journals and maps of Meriwether Lewis and William Clark, and in 2004 he paddled upstream to Bitterroot Mountain and stepped out onto the exact same trail they had completed on horseback, beginning in St. Louis, Missouri. In 199 days, he kayaked 2,400 miles up the Missouri River and backpacked over the Continental Divide.

"It took a while to get into the rhythm of rolling out of my tent every day to hike or paddle and then camp, again," he said. "But after two to three weeks, I felt like I'd gone back in time to find a place we've lost after two hundred years. Sometimes I got a chill down my back, realizing that I was in the same place that they had been."

Reentering the twenty-first century was not an easy transition, he says, but the in-depth knowledge he acquired has guided him in creating educational experiences at the Yellowstone Gateway Museum and organizing a fundraising campaign to place a statue of Sacagawea in a park in her name in Livingston, Montana. Living his dream placed him in a stream with many tributaries. Like John Colter, who returned to explore the Yellowstone region, Norm knows there is something yet to be discovered, or rediscovered, around the bend, and he's already on the trail.

Time Traveler: Norm contemplates past and present on the waters of the Yellowstone River in Livingston, Montana.

"Yellowstone opened up my artistic life to people from all over the world."

Carl Sheehan

Potter, resident artist at Old Faithful Lodge in Yellowstone National Park

Transforming a mound of clay into an object, such as a cup, a bowl, or even a teapot, looks like child's play when Carl is sitting behind his spinning potter's wheel, shaping and pulling up on the brown mass in the center with his muddy hands. That's because, after thirty-plus years of daily pottery making, it is easy for him. For twenty-seven of those years he worked in front of visitors every day from 9:00 A.M. to 5:00 P.M. all summer, making pottery and firing it in a gas kiln in the Old Faithful Lodge.

He began learning his craft in high school in Rochester, Minnesota. A wise teacher thought that Carl's teenage rowdiness could be channeled into something creative and introduced him to ceramics. It worked, and Carl continued to work with clay even after volunteering for the U.S. Marine Corps during the Vietnam War and being stationed in Hawaii and California.

After receiving his bachelor of arts degree from Montana State University, Carl worked as a potter in an art center in Bozeman from 1977 to 1980. He applied to be part of a new artist-in-the-park program in Yellowstone and was accepted.

Since then he and his wife have raised three children beside Old Faithful, and Carl has washed the clay off his hands to shake those of President Obama and former presidents Bill Clinton and Jimmy Carter. He enjoys meeting people and getting immediate feedback from visitors about his work. He has met other potters from all over the world and even shared his workbench with potters from Thailand and Luxembourg.

Mountains and Montana sunset scenes in stunning glazes of blue, red, and turquoise adorn many of his pieces, but his favorite design and creations are the buffalo pots, bison jars with lids, and tiny teacups. These days he is no longer making pots at the Old Faithful Lodge but rather is demonstrating the application of glazes and images. His creations are made in his Bozeman studio, Fire Hole Pottery Gallery, and amount to four to five tons of clay per year.

Carl says that he doesn't consciously try to come up with ideas for objects. Instead, he says, "I let them evolve on their own. If an idea is within me, it will emerge eventually."

With the beauty of Yellowstone for his eyes and the healing properties of thermal baths for his hands, Carl says he is where he needs to be, for his art, his body, and his soul.

Fire and Clay: Carl with a favorite pottery motif in his studio in Bozeman, Montana.

"Without wildness there can be no poets, no imagination, no fear."

Doug Smith

Project leader for wolf restoration project, biologist, ecologist

On January 12, 1995, at sunrise, a truck drove slowly through Roosevelt Arch at the north entrance to Yellowstone. Its cargo, which was probably not enjoying the ride, consisted of long-awaited celebrities that were finally coming home. Wolves had not been seen in the park since the last wolf was killed in 1926. Of the fifty-four wolves reintroduced in 1995, over five hundred of their descendants thrive in the Greater Yellowstone Ecosystem today.

Doug Smith, who had previously worked with wolves in Michigan and Minnesota, was there to welcome them and to champion their survival. Today, he supervises as many as twenty people who are dedicated to the philosophy that Yellowstone is a great conservation theater—one of the best in the world—and who are committed to keeping it that way. He is now studying the status of beaver, elk, and birds—especially swans, loons, and golden eagles—in the park. His one job with the Yellowstone Center for Resources has evolved into five different jobs.

Historically, the campaign against wolves began in the 1800s when westward expansion brought people and their livestock into areas occupied by wolves. As farmland expanded, the wolves' natural habitat and food sources were destroyed. Without prey, the wolves turned to domestic livestock for sustenance, resulting in retaliation by settlers. While rumors spread that wolves also preyed on humans, in fact wolves and humans can coexist peacefully when the relationship is managed and they can avoid one another.

Prejudice against wolves is still a strong sentiment, however, among those who live in areas surrounding the park. At the more than fifty talks Doug gives each year, people have no problem expressing how they feel, and he knows that people have strong feelings both for and against the wolves' reintroduction to the park. By being frank, open, and authentic, Doug articulates in these meetings why we need to preserve our "wildness" areas and the creatures, such as wolves, that live there.

"If we make the world into a human garden without wildness, without predators who belong there, we're creating an unnatural environment," he says. "A natural environment, which normally includes the wolf, requires its presence in order to be truly healthy. Wolves create a balance."

"In wildness is the preservation of the world. We need wild places to keep our humanity."

Alpha: Doug wrapped in a wolf skin he uses in lectures at the Lamar Buffalo Ranch, Yellowstone National Park, Wyoming.

"People have no idea how wild Yellowstone really is."

Erica Foley Trent

Backcountry ranger, U.S. Army veteran

Erica was moving hay bales on a ranch in Idaho, just back from a deployment in Iraq after sixteen years in the U.S. Army, when a friend suggested she might enjoy a summer job in Yellowstone National Park. She applied and, with her college degree in biology, experience growing up with horses, and recent role in public relations at the U.S. embassy in Iraq, discovered that she was uniquely qualified for the rigorous but exhilarating job of backcountry ranger.

"I became very familiar with using a chain saw and chopping wood—real quick!"

In the backcountry of Yellowstone, rangers travel on horseback to clear trails, move dead animals away from camping and hiking areas, answer questions from visitors, look for poachers or lost people, and deal with whatever else might happen unexpectedly in the wild.

"My job turned out to be one of those dreams that you think will never come true. I felt as if I'd gone back a hundred years to the real West."

Growing up in Michigan, Erica remembers watching the bears feed on garbage at the dump, but never had she experienced anything as wild as Yellowstone.

"There could be a bison right outside my tent, or cougar tracks."

While she was having her first experience with real wildness, she learned that visitors to the park also have limited knowledge of what it is like to be in an area with wild animals and potentially hazardous terrain. Reminding people to stay back from bison was a daily exercise, and questions such as, "What time do the bears come out?" or "Where will the wolves arrive?" made her realize that most people do not know how different a wild animal is from one that is domesticated or living in captivity.

In her present job as natural resource specialist for the U.S. Department of the Interior in Denver, Erica often thinks of her experiences at Yellowstone as she grapples with saving threatened species of wildlife and the environmental impact of abandoned coal mines.

When people ask her if she would return to life in the wilderness as a ranger—or if it might be right for them—she has sage advice: "I'd go back in a heartbeat, but, whatever I do, I always ask myself, Do I want to do it, and have I prepared myself to be safe?"

Back to Nature: Erica clearing trails in Yellowstone National Park.

"Museums must tell stories that include people."

Paul Shea

Yellowstone Gateway Museum curator

Back in 1979, when Paul first arrived in Yellowstone as a bus driver and tour guide from Reno, Nevada, he understood immediately that he had found the right place to live. "All I could say was, WOW! Something grabbed me. I knew this was where I belonged."

Since those early days, working in different locations in and around the park, Paul's enthusiasm for Yellowstone has never faltered. Today, he is able to combine both his love for place and his curiosity about people in his work as curator at the Yellowstone Gateway Museum.

Located in the historic North Side School in Livingston, Montana, the museum has collected a treasure trove of archives and objects pertaining to the history of Park County. The collection covers 12,000 years of human history with 50,000 items and is not about just "showing" history, but rather telling the stories of how, and from where, people arrived in the Park County area and how they survived. The exhibits cover four interpretive categories: Pioneers, Transportation, Expeditions, and Native Cultures. Archives include county voting registers from 1887 through 1940, City of Livingston business registers, the Polk Directories, and indexes of names from Park County newspapers. "As a museum, we are trying to help people place themselves in history. We want them to ask: How does what I've seen in that museum relate to my life?"

Among his favorite stories are those of Native Americans, the pioneer era, and the creation of small Chinese and Japanese populations in the area. "We want to pose the question of why people wanted to get up and leave the East Coast and come here, and how migration from other countries on the other side of the world began. How did they survive here?" The museum's exhibitions have invited visitors to follow the journey of Lewis and Clark and experience the evolution of transportation in Park County. Local schools can check out a teaching trunk that explores handmade tools used by early Native American cultures; or understand bison from a market perspective as food, clothing, and jewelry; or approach history through topographical maps that show Montana and its seven reservations.

Paul enjoys a good story with a cast of characters and follows the advice that a story must have a beginning, a middle, and an end—but not necessarily in that order. The most important element is people: who they are and how they landed in any particular story.

Living History: Paul, in front of Yellowstone Gateway Museum, stands on the caboose that once traveled to the Gardiner, Montana, train station.

"I'm proud of my contributions toward our understanding of Yellowstone birds."

Terry McEneaney

Yellowstone ornithologist, mountaineer

Terry McEneaney is a rare species (of human). During over four decades of watching and studying birds in Yellowstone, he has contributed more to the understanding and knowledge of bird conservation than almost any other single individual. His observations and monitoring over the years, have contributed to the preservation of the peregrine falcon and bald eagle.

Besides his continuous research, he has educated and trained thousands of tour guides, interpreters, students, and the public about Yellowstone birds and their conservation.

But where did such extraordinary dedication to the world of birdlife begin? For Terry, it may have been in the deciduous forests of New Hampshire, where he grew up near one of the greatest bird taxidermy collections in New England, the Wentworth Collection, a nearby neighbor in his hometown. It may also have been in his name. The family name McEneaney is of Gaelic derivation, and one translation is "son of the birdman." So, not surprisingly, Terry's roots go back to 1368 in Ireland, where his ancestors were purportedly gamekeepers.

As a child, Terry's love for birds was reinforced by his father's experience with bird hunting and his mother's enthusiasm to drive Terry around in her car watching birds. Terry's older brother, an intrepid traveler, nudged him to leave the familiarity of New Hampshire birdlife and attend college in the American West. Terry migrated to Montana, where he climbed every mountain range and studied everything ranging from songbirds to raptors. He conducted bird surveys throughout Montana, Wyoming, and Colorado—one of his favorite climbs is Eagle Peak, the tallest mountain in Yellowstone—and sixteen major mountains in the Alps.

Besides his passion for Yellowstone birds and field ornithology, he has searched and studied birds in Ireland, Wales, Scotland, Greenland, Mexico, Alaska, Argentina, and Chile, but the birds of Yellowstone are the crown jewels of his vast collective knowledge and experience.

Reaching back to his childhood upbringing, he recites from Robert Frost's poem "The Road Not Taken": "Two roads diverged in a wood, and I— / I took the one less traveled by, / And that has made all the difference." In bird conservation, Terry has made significant contributions to our knowledge of many bird species, and he's honored to hold the distinguished title Ornithologist Emeritus of Yellowstone National Park. "The road I chose allowed me to express my true talents and field skills. I realize a career like mine is rare in today's world. My cup is full."

Birdman: Terry McEneaney is an expert/author on birds in the Yellowstone ecosystem.

"Our effort to control invasive trout species has benefited from people remembering the good old days when the lake was full of beautiful cutthroat trout. Visitors wanted them back."

Pat Bigelow

National Park Service fishery biologist

For those parents who wonder if a loosely organized summer of travel to parts unknown can be good for a college student, Pat Bigelow definitely answers in the affirmative. She will also admit that she had never heard of Yellowstone National Park during her childhood growing up on a dairy farm with six siblings in northern Vermont. The discovery came when she arrived in Bozeman, Montana, for a summer job in 1979 and eventually joined the Young Adult Conservation Corps. That first season included a week participating in fishery research on Yellowstone Lake and set her career on course.

In 2001, she returned as an official fish biologist after fifteen years of working for the U.S. Fish and Wildlife Service, equipped with the education and experience required to enter what was soon to be a prototype battle against an invasive species.

On her return to Yellowstone, she discovered that lake trout had been feeding on the native cutthroat trout almost to the point of extinction. Although lake trout (which are tasty fish and may be caught) were introduced to select waters of Yellowstone National Park some time around the end of the nineteenth century, they are thought to have been introduced into Yellowstone Lake in the 1980s. It was several years later that fish researchers—and fishermen—began to notice a decline in cutthroat trout. Perhaps the grizzlies had noticed, too, because spawning cutthroat are one of the most important food sources for bears and more than forty other animal species.

Pat remembers that, in 1979, during her first work on Yellowstone Lake, the cutthroat, with their distinctive red markings, were extremely abundant. When she returned in 2001, she says, "The contrast was shocking. The beautiful, bright-colored trout were barely present." The good news is that fish biologists like Pat feel a simple solution is working to slow the population of the invader: Teams of people are now working to catch the lake trout in specially designed gill nets in order to reduce their numbers substantially and quickly. She loves being on the lake, working daily to catch and monitor the fish. Native species caught in the nets are carefully handled, studied, and returned. She believes that, with time and enough nets, the balance may return to normal.

Pat is optimistic that Yellowstone Lake and its tributaries will soon glisten with the essential cutthroat trout, and she attributes the program's success, in part, to the support of people who remember the abundance of those flashy fish from years ago—and want them back.

Net Catch: Netting invasive trout species on Yellowstone Lake.

"Every scientist who visited Yellowstone had a story to tell, and I was there to listen."

John Varley

Former director of Yellowstone Center for Resources, fishery biologist

When John Varley's parents honeymooned in Yellowstone in the 1930s, little did they know that their child would grow up to become a leader of resource stewardship within the National Park Service. John, now in his seventies, recalls visiting Yellowstone at the age of six. "I can still remember the wonder of the place. We stayed in old wooden cabins with no heat. Bears were everywhere and being fed by hand. With buffalo, elk, and fish—it was paradise for a kid."

John and his wife carried on the tradition, honeymooning in Yellowstone and eventually raising three sons, all of whom have the pleasure of saying, "I grew up in Yellowstone."

He was working with the U.S. Fish and Wildlife Service in the early 1980s when he received a call inviting him to apply for chief of science research at Yellowstone. He knew it would be the world's best job for him because of his love of science. As he began to oversee park biologists and geologists as well as issue annual permits to visiting scientists, he quickly realized that each day would be a feast of information—and he was never disappointed.

"One day I'm listening to a dung fungus scientist describe the life cycle of a fungus that depends on being swallowed by an elk and passing through five stomachs, and the next day a geophysicist studying the Yellowstone 'hot spot' drops by with his work. After that it might be a bird guy."

John pushed for the application of science to solve preservation and conservation issues in the park, impressing upon potential researchers within the Yellowstone ecosystem the need to pursue rigorous and reportable science. He also ensured that the results of scientific studies were translated into everyday language for the public's consumption in publications like *Yellowstone Science*. "Naturalists started sharing stories, and people love scientists who can speak in layman's terms."

John's use and promotion of science to improve resource preservation has changed public attitudes and facilitated the evolution of National Park Service policies. When resolving problems as diverse as invasive lake trout, bison, wolves, and bears, John has listened first and then directed his energies and information in the appropriate directions. When asked about his favorite spot in the park, he said, "I have about two hundred of them. It depends on the day of the year. On July 4, it's the top of Mount Washburn. Those wildflowers are the Yellowstone magic show."

Dedicated to Science: John has been involved with every aspect of scientific investigation in Yellowstone.

"If wolves get used to you, they may come and steal your shoes."

Linda Thurston

Yellowstone wolf tracker, biologist

Wolf dens are cozy places, so much so that they may even attract other beasts when the original residents vacate the premises. Since April 1, 1996, just after wolves were reintroduced to Yellowstone National Park, Linda Thurston has been observing all aspects of wolf behavior and especially what happens in their dens.

"I was so lucky to be there when the wolves arrived in Yellowstone. But they wouldn't come out of their pens right away. We had to lure them out with roadkill meat."

Since then she has worked for many years on the wolf project and spent many long days spotting wolf packs using radio telemetry. It was on one of these long days of wolf tracking that she discovered a small homeless black bear snuggled in an abandoned wolf den.

"Wolves are excellent home builders. Their dens are usually a tunnel with an entrance above and below marked by a large pile of dirt, and they're often reused by generations of wolves. They are often near a source of water and are kept very clean. Other animals usually avoid wolves, but an abandoned den is pretty enticing."

Hours of observation have provided Linda with a unique insight into the family lifestyles and pack behavior of wolves. After following the Druid pack for several years, Linda says that she knows them like her own dogs. Wolves are curious about humans, too. "They have gotten used to us in some areas and they'll move in closer to check us out. We can't see them always, but we spot them by radio signal."

From observations of den behavior, Linda has learned that wolves know their offspring and every wolf in the pack has a specific job. In the past, researchers thought that young females didn't contribute substantially to the pack, but wolf watchers today know that yearling females are often the designated babysitters.

Linda loves to share the thrill of spotting and observing wolves and other wildlife with visitors. "It's exciting to come upon an animal and be able to talk about where it fits in the family group. We do more than just identify them by their markings. We know their individual personalities. Male wolves usually hold down the territory. Females make other decisions, but watch out for those youngsters. They can be especially curious."

Wolf Woman: Linda curls up in an abandoned wolf den in Yellowstone National Park.

"I believe in saving the environment, one bottle or can at a time."

Wendy Medina

Recycler, artist, hiker

"You're not throwing that out, are you? I know someone who might be able to use part of that to fix a bicycle."

Everyone who knew Wendy during her six years as Yellowstone's recycling expert in the Old Faithful maintenance yard has heard this question in some form—probably many times. "I was always nice about it," she says. "But people need to be educated about recycling."

Recycling education and the physical act of recycling became her passion after a short stint as a waitress in the Old Faithful Inn. By chance, her predecessor in charge of recycling retired, and the strenuous and endless job of driving "Old Yeller," the 1963 yellow milk truck used as the official recycling vehicle, became available. She jumped at the chance to drive around all day from the inn to the Snow Lodge to the gift shop to staff housing and parts unknown to pick up glass, plastic, paper, metal, and old appliances, always with a smile and friendly suggestion of how to dispose of things properly.

Wendy also speaks German and Spanish, increasing her ability to communicate with as many people as possible about the benefits of recycling. "If you make it easy for people, they'll get on board with the idea."

She proceeded to reorganize her job to maximize recycling throughout the park and rode her bike, made from recycled parts, to recreation areas in her off-hours, "just to pick things up and put them in the right bins."

Keeping up with the consuming demands of her job while also saving the world, one bottle at a time, however, meant that she missed having enough time for serious hiking. So, her dream is return to Yellowstone, just to hike and enjoy the park as a visitor. But it's certain that she may have some questions for other hikers along the trail, like: "What are you planning to do with that can when you're finished with it?"

If you don't have a plan, she'll help you with that.

Dirty Job: Wendy unloads cardboard for recycling in Yellowstone National Park.

"In a rescue operation I feel like one piece of an incredible machine."

Jack McConnell

Member of the Jenny Lake "Climbing Rangers" mountain rescue team, three-time recipient of the U.S. Department of the Interior Valor Award for heroism

Mountain climbing is one of the most thrilling of all outdoor sports, requiring strength, precision, good judgment, and, most importantly, knowledge of the terrain. When Jack McConnell arrived in Livingston, Montana, on a Greyhound bus as a teenager, he was already a skilled climber from years of climbing in the White Mountains of New Hampshire in his native New England, but he didn't know the Tetons and all the peaks of the Yellowstone region.

Not only would he become master of every mountain in the area; he also established a reputation for speed and is known as "Jack Hammer" or "Hydraulic Jack," the guy with pistons for legs. His personal best time for the 2,170-foot climb from Lower Saddle to the summit of Grand Teton is fifty-five minutes. The same route takes most climbers eight hours or more. Knowing many of the climbing routes in the Yellowstone region is also a qualifying prerequisite for members of the elite Jenny Rangers, with whom Jack has worked in rescue operations for more than twenty years.

Jack says, "There are no pretensions about survival when we go out. A helicopter drops us into rough terrain that we hope to get out of with whomever we are rescuing, but there is never a guarantee. The spotter and pilot will make the decision as to whether they have to abandon the mission."

He is proud to be part of one of the best rescue teams in the world. As physically fit as world-class athletes, they are a mixture of skilled firefighters, emergency medical personnel, law enforcement officers, riggers of rescue equipment, helicopter pilots, and, above all, climbers.

Lightning strikes, falls, crumbling rocks, and lost people are among the many events that can initiate a rescue operation. "They don't pay us for what we do, but for the potential of what we can do."

His three visits to the White House to receive medals of valor for heroism resulted from rescues that occurred under horrific conditions. In one case, as many as eighteen climbers had been struck by lightning in the Grand Tetons and were scattered over the mountain in different places suffering from paralysis, cardiac arrest, and entering and exiting wounds.

Jack says, "We respond to everything—even people who just get tired. When we show up for work each day, we never know what might happen, but it's the best job in the world working with the best people in the world."

Lifesaver: Jack just after a death-defying mountain rescue operation.

"To become superintendent of Yellowstone is an opportunity that doesn't come along very often."

Dan Wenk

Yellowstone National Park superintendent, landscape architect

When Dan Wenk started working at the National Park Service's Denver Service Center, planning and designing construction projects for Yellowstone, he never imagined how deeply he would become involved in managing Yellowstone. In 1979, however, he and his family were relocated to Lower Mammoth and the love story began in earnest.

With a degree in landscape architecture from Michigan State University, Dan was well qualified to meet the challenge of dealing with the park's deteriorating buildings and reducing their burden on the landscape with less, and lighter, architecture. In his first Yellowstone experience he worked under two superintendents during five years, with the mission of developing designs that were sensitive to the park's preservation. Little did he know that thirty years later he would find himself in the ultimate position of responsibility. During the intervening years he worked in several other parks, and he feels that Yellowstone is different, not only because of the size and abundance of resources, diverse wildlife, and unique geothermal features, but also because its preservation is reliant on an incredible ecosystem that includes the numerous national forests of Montana, Wyoming, and Idaho and their management.

"Leaders in conservation all over the world are looking at how Yellowstone is being protected. We have a big responsibility to represent a high standard of preservation. And the issues are constantly changing. Thirty years ago we were not as concerned about management outside park boundaries. Now we know that the preservation of Yellowstone's natural resources, especially wildlife, is dependent on the surrounding areas. Wildlife do not respect political boundaries."

Just a few of the other issues Dan is facing at the helm of Yellowstone are maintaining vigilance in the battle against nonnative lake trout species, the growing increase in visitors each year (now more than 4 million), and how to balance resource protection with high-quality visitor experiences, along with monitoring climate change effects. There are also the issues relating to bison, wolves, bear, winter use of the park—the list goes on—but Dan is glad he has arrived at a place where he has the opportunity to make a difference, and he's honored to be in a position where he is truly responsible for the long-term preservation and use of Yellowstone.

Dan says, "It's not so bad to live in a place where you can hear an owl outside your window instead of a siren."

Buck Stops Here: Dan stands in front of a three-dimensional map showing the landscape elevations of Yellowstone National Park.

"A museum should be a living, breathing place where we understand the lessons of the past to help shape our future."

Charles R. Preston, PhD

Wildlife biologist, museum curator, director, educator

Charles Preston's dream about what a natural history museum should be in the twenty-first century led him to fulfill an early, youthful promise. He first visited Yellowstone in the early 1970s, on a typical post-high school road trip with friends. Awestruck by the park's beauty and natural wonders, he commented, "Someday, I'm going to live here."

His eventual career as a university professor of biology and ecology took him on many paths, but one of the pathways leading to his dream location led through the Denver Museum of Natural History, where Charles was offered a job as curator and zoology department chairman. This path brought him to the Rocky Mountains. He was subsequently recruited to lead the design and development of the Draper Museum of Natural History at the Buffalo Bill Center of the West in Cody, Wyoming. This brought him next to the east entrance of Yellowstone National Park. The Draper Museum is focused on exploring and interpreting the nature and science of Yellowstone and the surrounding region.

Charles' perspective on the role of a museum curator goes far beyond the traditional definition. At the Draper, his guiding principle was to present scientific information in a way that would integrate the world of the museum's research and collections and data with the life of the community and beyond. His goal was to be a full-service museum and to make the products of original scientific research accessible to everyone through broad educational outreach. The scientific collections of the Draper serve as a permanent record of life in the Greater Yellowstone region and are used by scientists and educators around the globe. "Yellowstone National Park can neither contain nor sustain viable populations of the charismatic wildlife living here. These animals move in and out of the park, and their conservation depends on understanding their needs, the needs of landowners outside the park, and potential conflicts between the two."

Charles believes that Yellowstone's wildlife can continue to flourish if we understand wildlife through science and socioeconomic needs of landowners through open communication. He says, "Museum activities should empower our visitors and constituents with the knowledge needed to conserve Greater Yellowstone and shape its future for people and wildlife." As one high school student said after a community education program, "I always took so much granted. I'll look a lot closer from now on."

"Music to my ears," said Charles.

Legacy: Charles and nonreleasable educational rescue bird Kateri, a golden eagle, in Cody, Wyoming.

"People assume that Yellowstone will always be here, but that's true only if we take care of it."

Margie Fey

National park ranger, aquatic invasive species inspector

During her early days as a health and physical education teacher looking for a summer adventure in 1975 with her husband, Rick Fey, Margie never imagined that she would work from turf to surf at Yellowstone National Park, at first perched high in a fire tower on Mount Washburn watching for forest fires, followed by twenty-five years in law enforcement, and moving eventually to resource management inspecting boats that might carry invasive aquatic species. Preventing the introduction of nonnative (from another continent or outside their normal range) aquatic species has become a passion for Margie. "People don't realize how easy it is to bring a tiny hitchhiker along in the crevice of a boat when they've been boating in other waterways outside the park."

Aquatic invasive species pose significant dangers to Yellowstone's ecological processes. If a nonnative species has no natural predators in its adopted environment, its population may increase rapidly and threaten the native species, causing a native species to become extinct, with the highest extinction rates occurring in freshwater environments. In addition to nonnative fish in Yellowstone, three more aquatic invasive species are having a significant detrimental effect in the park.

Myxobolus cerebralis, a parasite that causes whirling disease in cutthroat trout and other species; New Zealand mud snails, which form dense colonies and compete with native species; and red-rimmed melania, a small snail that was first imported by the aquarium trade in the 1930s and was discovered in the warm swimming area at the confluence of the Boiling and Gardner Rivers in 2009.

Eliminating aquatic invasive species after they become established in a watershed is usually impossible and extremely expensive. Each summer Margie is part of a small team of park technicians who inspect, decontaminate, and air-dry visitors' boats and angling gear before they can be placed in the water. Such decontamination is usually adequate to prevent the entry of most aquatic invasive species. She reminds people that it is illegal to use any fish as bait in Yellowstone National Park, and it's also illegal to transport fish from one river or lake to another in the Yellowstone region.

During the years in which Margie returned to the classroom each fall, she says the Yellowstone experience created a remarkable increase in her skills as a teacher.

"It's been a marvelous journey of learning and satisfaction that I'm contributing to the future of this wonderful place."

Cleanup Time: Margie holds a spray gun used to clean and disinfect boats headed for Yellowstone waters.

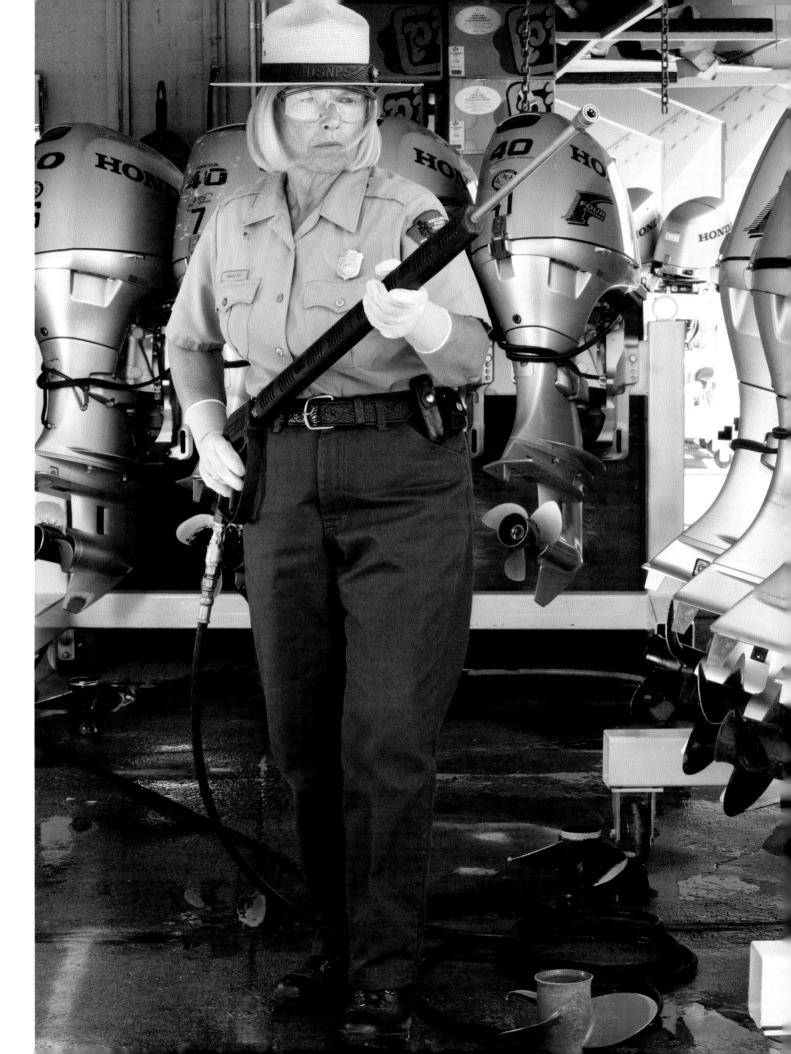

"Humans can learn a lot from trees."

John King

Dendrochronologist, ecologist

When John King hugs a tree, it's more than a passing fancy. He knows that trees can be used to study almost anything from the exact age of a painting by a Dutch master, to the date when a violin was made in the fifteenth century, to a span of time when a stream changed its course, causing the growth or death of trees.

For John, the discovery of dendrochronology—using tree rings to answer questions about the natural world—was a chance encounter that transformed his life. While majoring in watershed management at the University of Arizona and touring the laboratory of tree-ring research located in the football stadium, he realized the study of tree rings involved a set of skills that excited him and he was hooked. In 2000 he launched a consulting firm, Lone Pine Research, to provide expertise based on tree-ring data.

"It's not just about counting tree rings," John says. "It's about using the principles and techniques of dendrochronology to determine the exact year of formation of each ring." Such data is used in a wide variety of research projects.

Tree-ring research can be used to determine the age of cultural artifacts, the timing of tree establishment and death, the timing and effects of climate change, and the frequency and extent of floods and fires, and much more. John has used buried deadwood remnants to precisely date a volcanic eruption that occurred in 1350 C.E. and fire scars on lodgepole pines to examine the characteristics of prehistoric fire events.

When John observed axe-cut stumps in a photograph, he knew he could use the stumps to identify the exact location where the Nez Perce tribe had stayed in Yellowstone when they traveled through, escaping the U.S. Army. This research finding gives substance to an important episode in U.S. history.

Collecting records of tree growth is not always a stroll in the woods, however. In order to make 3,000-year tree-ring records, numerous deadwood samples are required. This involves conducting research activities on foot, with permission from the Park Service, in remote settings with no trails and no people while carrying many pounds of equipment—saws, borers, GPS, strapping tape, food, water—and returning with up to a hundred pounds of tree-ring samples.

"This may reflect my heritage," John says. "My ancient Norwegian ancestors had the task of carrying back heavy slabs of meat to their camp. I'm carrying history, hidden in a tree."

Tree-Ring Counter: John blends in with tree branches on a 1,000-year-old juniper in Yellowstone National Park.

"All horses are different, just like people."

Ethan Perry

Farrier, mechanical engineer

No job in the world requires more "horse sense" than the job performed by the men and women who spend their days bent over next to a horse, clipping, rasping, nipping, and cutting the hooves of horses and finally applying a new shoe. While horses vary in their tolerance of this essential activity, farriers like Ethan Perry know that horses understand, for the most part, and cooperate.

By examining a horse's hooves as he trims and cleans them and applies new shoes every six weeks, Ethan instantly knows a lot about the health and comfort of the horse. Unhealthy hooves and uneven, poorly fitted shoes can shorten a horse's life.

"Domesticated horses, like those used for trail rides in Yellowstone, need horseshoes because their hooves don't wear themselves down as much as [the hooves of] a wild horse. Trail-ride horses are walking on softer surfaces, and they also need shoes for traction in slippery conditions."

Ethan's career with horses in Yellowstone started when he was eight years old working alongside his father, Dick Perry. After taking time out for college to become a mechanical engineer, he returned to the demanding job of farrier. Work is steady, even through the winter.

Besides cleaning and trimming hooves, a farrier acts as a blacksmith and removes old shoes, bends shoes to the proper shape (usually by heating shoes in a forge), and then nails the shoes in place. "Most of this takes place while standing and bent over at the waist, bracing the horse's leg between my legs. It took my back a few years to get used to holding this position all day."

The constant physical closeness to the horse makes farriers attentive to the quirks and personality differences between the animals. "Some need a little more time. They know how they want to be handled." And what about all those mountains of used horseshoes? Ethan says they just become art projects. "You should see the things that people make out of them."

Ethan says horseshoeing is much more fun than it looks. "I love horses; they are wonderful creatures to work with and I work in a beautiful place. There are a lot of rewards in what I do."

Carrying on Tradition: Ethan and his father have put new shoes on thousands of horses.

"Restoring historic Yellowstone, one miniature building at a time."

Vic Sawyer

Master model builder, snow coach driver, hotel and store manager

When architects use the expression "the devil is in the details" during the building design process, they may have coined the best way to describe the painstaking work of Vic Sawyer as he wrestles with the devilish task of reducing a gigantic building to perfect, tabletop scale. His appreciation for details led him into a hobby of staggering architectural complexity—in miniature. These are not dollhouses but magnificent recreations of historic Yellowstone structures. Vic's first project, Lake Lodge, a 1:300 scale model, allows the viewer to take in all the grandeur in one glimpse of the nineteenth-century hotel listed on the National Register of Historic Places. His model even twinkles with tiny incandescent lights shining through its windows.

In other details of Vic's life, he has driven snow coaches during the "magnificent Yellowstone winters" and managed hotels and the Haynes Photo Shop, where the work of F. Jay Haynes and his son, Jack, are displayed. A successful appearance on the quiz show *Jeopardy* in 2007 also revealed that Vic is quick on his feet with lots of information—a useful talent when responding to visitors in his work with the Yellowstone Foundation (now known as Yellowstone Forever).

One of his recent modeling projects is that of the elegant Canyon Hotel, built in 1911 but torn down in 1960 to make way for the more modest Canyon Village units, also eventually replaced by smaller lodges. Vic has worked on the model of the hotel, relying mainly on photographs and anecdotal descriptions. For materials he uses thin sheets of wood, along with an assortment of tiny wooden objects, carefully painted, from coffee stirrers to toothpicks.

Vic's magnificent models are the ultimate, carefully wrought depictions of Yellowstone's architectural history. Let's hope he tackles the Old Faithful Inn!

History in the Making: Vic sets the roof on his scale-model replica of Yellowstone's Lake Lodge.

"Don't be afraid to try something new. Start doing it and go with it."

Nicola Grupido

Manager of housekeeping at Lake Lodge, aspiring writer

Besides rangers, trail guides, and people high up on fire lookout towers, hundreds of seasonal workers make life comfortable for visitors staying in Yellowstone's many hotels, lodges, and cabins.

Growing up in Michigan and looking for a summer job, Nicola wasn't interested in pursuing the art of making beds, cleaning bathrooms, and delivering fresh towels, but when a friend told him about the wildlife and beauty of Yellowstone, he quickly applied online and landed a position in the housekeeping department in a hotel within the park.

"I was very shy," he says. "But I met people from all over the world and I enjoyed the teamwork involved. It was a great confidence booster." Soon he was promoted to assistant manager of housekeeping at Lake Lodge.

Housekeepers also get a glimpse into the private lives of hotel guests. Besides the usual assortment of mobile phone and computer chargers, strange notes written on scraps of paper, food wrappers, and the occasional weapon that are left behind, one visitor left a bookmark made entirely of elephant dung. Nicola has found dogs left in rooms and once came face-to-face with a 2,000-pound bison just outside a door. His favorite part of the job was meeting a diverse group of employees and figuring out how to work with them. Yellowstone attracts workers from all over the world.

"In my off-time, I hiked and backpacked. Electric Peak was one of my favorite places."

Nicola says that the sense of community among park employees is the best of anywhere he's ever worked, and hiking was a great way to get to know people. "All I had to do was ask if anyone would like to take a hike, and five people would jump up and say, 'Let's go!'"

Today, besides his managerial duties at Lake Lodge, Nicola is pursuing a career in writing and is grateful for the unforgettable experiences he encountered in Yellowstone—both inside and outside. He hopes one day to be writing about his experience.

Man Behind the Scenes: Nicola attempts to perform one of the many tasks related to housekeeping at Lake Lodge, Yellowstone.

"Now I know what the song 'America the Beautiful' is all about."

Caroline McClure

Retail sales manager at Lake Hotel gift shop

There is no question that Yellowstone National Park is a magnet for talented people ready and willing to work in a variety of jobs. They find their way to the park for an equally wide variety of reasons. Educated in fine art, Caroline was working in an art gallery in Texas in 2004 when she realized that a complete change in location and lifestyle could happen if she was ready to take the risk. Growing up in Wisconsin, she had skied since age fourteen. She also had a fond memory of a visit to Yellowstone as a child with her parents and siblings, and another at age twenty-seven with her husband.

She had sold or given away her accumulated belongings before embarking for Yellowstone and "didn't know a soul" when she arrived for her first job as a ski guide in Mammoth Hot Springs. Soon she was setting up and staffing a trailer for ski and snowshoe rentals and taking ski tour groups into gorgeous locales along the canyon. From her Norwegian ancestry she had brought *friluftsliv* along from Texas, a word to describe someone who needs solitude in nature to clarify thoughts and feelings about the future.

During the next summer, her job as a retail associate in the Lake Hotel gift shop was an entirely different challenge but also the best one so far, and soon she was moving up in managerial responsibility.

"Life is so varied and fun in a gift shop—especially in a historic hotel. The staff becomes a family, with a core group that returns year after year, along with interesting new people, both young and old. Our mission, besides selling, is to listen to visitors, and we often hear the same story over and over, the same amazement at the beauty of the place."

With her love for landscape, Caroline enjoys walking in the sand along the edge of the lake or hiking through fields up to Storm Point. Many of her friends in her Yellowstone "family" are musicians, and social life revolves around listening to members of a string quartet who play regularly in the sunroom of the hotel.

Two of her colleagues were recently married in the same hotel sunroom. Fly-fishing was the wedding theme, and the guests came wearing waders, vests, and hats.

As Caroline looks forward to her next season in the gift shop, she reflects: "Now I live with many layers of friendship, beauty, history, and landscape. I've learned a lot about myself here."

Memories: Caroline relaxes in front of the fireplace at Lake Lodge in Yellowstone.

"I get plenty of exercise moving nine hundred bales of hay each week."

Fred Ersepke

Yellowstone National Park horse department employee

Back in 1975, Fred Ersepke was driving city and school buses in La Crosse, Wisconsin, while attending college, when he saw an ad for bus drivers needed in Yellowstone National Park. "Why not?" he said, and he embarked on a lifelong career in "the most picturesque place [he'd] ever seen."

In 1975–76, Yellowstone Park Company purchased twenty-five new buses for transporting visitors within the park. They recruited many young, enthusiastic college students with bus driving experience, like Fred, from around the country. After a few seasons, Fred moved on to the dispatch department and maintenance, taking care of Yellowstone vehicles from buses to snowmobiles and other winter transportation. Eventually he took on the job of running the five warehouses from which all of the supplies used in the park are distributed. Six days a week he drove a semi tractor-trailer truck into the park loaded with food, paper supplies, and everything else needed to operate the hotels, gift shops, and concessions.

"You can go through a lot of toilet paper when you have 2 million to 3 million visitors a year," he says.

Today Fred spends his summers working with the horse department. Yellowstone has approximately three hundred horses used for trail rides in Canyon Village along with stagecoach trips and horseback rides out to cowboy cookouts at Roosevelt Lodge near the Lamar Valley. Fred works with a team who bring the horses down from their winter pasture area, check them for veterinary problems, and shoe them. Once the horses are in their stalls and back to work, Fred hauls in nine hundred bales of hay each week. He also helps to muck out the stalls daily and load the straw-and-manure mixture back on a truck that he drives to a gravel pit, where it is mixed with soil to reclaim the hillside.

"It's been a wonderful life in a beautiful place," Fred says. "I never need to take a vacation because I live in one of the most spectacular places in America. I can hardly believe that I've already been here more than forty years—and I'm aiming for fifty."

Horse Country: Fred enjoys the beauty of Yellowstone while taking care of Yellowstone National Park horses.

"How we care for visitors to Yellowstone is a metaphor for how we care for the park."

Katy Duffy

Yellowstone National Park ranger, educator, raptor specialist

If you ask Katy about the happiest moments of her thirty-two years as a resource education ranger and interpretive planner, she will undoubtedly reflect back on the times when she was able to work directly with visitors, teaching them how to read the landscape of the park or taking them on a night walk to help them feel more comfortable in the wild. Katy says, "Helping visitors to grasp the significance of and enjoy their national park safely has always been my favorite part of my job."

Her proudest moment was the opportunity to host the First Family on their visit to Old Faithful in 2009. She spent almost an hour with the Obama family, describing the geological features and natural history of the area. "I was petrified beforehand but immediately became relaxed with their warm, courteous, and intelligent questions and comments."

"When the president asked me if the park had planted all those trees that have grown up in the areas burned by the fires of 1988, I had the chance to describe how the lodgepole pine seeds are naturally sealed with a waxy resin and melt open by fire. It was delightful to see him turn and explain it in his own terms to his children."

Retirement has given Katy new opportunities. She now shares her extensive knowledge of birds through the Yellowstone Raptor Initiative, which inventories and monitors select raptor species—such as golden eagles, red-tailed hawks, Swainson's hawks, American kestrels, prairie falcons, and owls—from among the nineteen breeding raptor species supported by the park.

Katy has worked with owls as a licensed bird-bander since 1979 and even travels back to her home state of New Jersey to band owls to get her "bird fix." She uses sound to attract owls and applies ID bands to yield important knowledge about migration, breeding, and habitats.

She has a ready answer when asked what has been the best thing about being a ranger. "Living in the park! We get paid in sunsets—and more."

Taking Care: Katy stands in front of Old Faithful in Yellowstone, where she served as a park ranger from 2002 to 2011.

"I consider the mountainside a special place."

Doug Peacock

Vietnam War veteran, writer, naturalist, filmmaker

For those who return from war, nothing is ever the same again. Doug Peacock spent two tours of duty in Vietnam as a medic with the Green Berets. He came back speechless from what he had witnessed and set off on an odyssey of immersion in nature and retreat from human contact. As he describes in his memoir, *Grizzly Years: In Search of the American Wilderness,* "I had trouble with a world whose idea of vitality was anything other than the naked authenticity of living or dying. The world paled, as did all my life before, and I found myself estranged from my own time."

He did have his curiosity intact, though, and decided to follow it wherever it might lead. For Doug, this meant looking for wild places, or at least trying to discover what was left of them in the natural world. A recurrence of malaria led him to Yellowstone National Park, traveling from the Wind River area. "I thought the weather might be better."

There are few publicly recognized heroes from the Vietnam War, but Doug became one to other veterans and to a group of environmentalists when he became Edward Abbey's model for the character Hayduke in *The Monkey Wrench Gang,* published in 1975. Hayduke never recovers from the trauma of war, but Doug was led toward healing when he decided to spend solitary time in wild country observing grizzly bears in a place where humans were not the dominant creature.

His years of observation and careful calculation about what is required to live and survive in the wild restored his relationship with himself. His experience and storytelling ability force readers to examine their own uses of wilderness and the human need to control the environment. His mission is to fight for the wildness that is left in the world. As an author and cofounder of Round River Conservation Studies, he travels throughout the world to work with indigenous people to help preserve native wildlands (25 million acres of big wilderness protected so far). He has written about surviving in the wild, global warming, the death of the Pleistocene megafauna, the disappearance of today's ice, and his experience advocating for the preservation of wilderness.

When he's not traveling, Doug lives in Paradise Valley, Montana, just north of Yellowstone, where he can stay abreast of environmental and wildlife issues related to the preservation of the park. He expresses his feeling of responsibility simply: "Yellowstone—that's my job."

Witness to the Earth: Doug Peacock has spent the last fifty years wandering the earth's wildest places.

"There is nothing more satisfying than getting as close to the rising trout as possible, whether slowly sliding along the bank on my butt or wade-walking in the river on my knees."

Craig Mathews

Professional fly-fishing guide, author

Mastering the art of fly-fishing has been a lifelong journey for Craig Mathews. His fascination with the sport began at the age of four, when his parents first started taking him and his brother to Silver Lake near their home in Grand Rapids, Michigan. This was also the moment in time when Craig began to experience the spirit of sharing and teaching that is characteristic among people who are passionate about fly-fishing.

Craig recalls being a child, wandering with his broken fishing pole out to a lineup of fishermen on the lake next to his family's summer cottage, when one man motioned him over and gave him a short casting lesson. With only a few casts, he caught a four-inch bluegill; after only a few more catches, he was hooked on fly-fishing for life.

Many years and fishing experiences later, Craig and his wife, Jackie, relocated to West Yellowstone, with Craig working as police chief and Jackie as police dispatcher. In the 1970s they launched Blue Ribbon Flies, a fishing guide service, and by 1980 they had hired handicapped workers to tie flies. When Craig retired from police work in 1982, he also turned over the wholesale operation of Blue Ribbon Flies to his handicapped staff.

His deep sense of philanthropy and passion for conservation have continued through his work with One Percent for the Planet, an alliance of 1,500 businesses that donate 1 percent of their gross income to approved conservation and preservation projects. Craig has also found a way to incorporate the blue ribbon trout streams of Yellowstone into his philanthropy by recently donating two days of guided fishing to benefit the Madison River Foundation Project, which focuses on conservation and preservation.

Craig believes that "fly-fishing helps preserve our capacity for wonder." Over the years, he went from "fishing dry flies exclusively to solely fishing nymphs, then to streamers, and back to fishing dry flies again." His goal is to share the simplest approaches to fly-fishing to enable children, the handicapped, and disabled veterans an opportunity to experience success.

Preserving Nature: Craig supports many projects focused on preservation, like this high-elevation fish hatchery.

"I like to meet people but not necessarily on a search mission, because they're lost."

Bonnie Whitman Gafney

National Park Service ranger, search-and-rescue dog handler, coroner

"There's nothing worse than looking for lost kids," says Bonnie while describing her thirty-four years of working in law enforcement in six different national parks. Over those years she has trained four dogs in the demanding art of searching for lost people and sniffing out drugs. "It's all about hunting," she says. "Some dogs are easier to train than others. Training includes not only finding someone or something, but shaping their behavior to bring the handler back to the subject after they complete their hunt."

Teaching children (and adults) how not to get lost in the first place is also one of Bonnie's specialties. She teaches kids the Hug-a-Tree program in schools and parks, hoping to instill a knowledge base that may last a lifetime. She teaches them to observe landmarks as they walk by, how to be aware of leaving good tracks, and—most importantly—to stay put and "hug a tree" if they become lost. She gives demonstrations with her search-and-rescue dog, a friendly German shepherd named Gator, who is fourth in a successful line of search dogs. Bonnie says she loves walking around park campgrounds, talking to visitors and introducing her dog to kids.

"I've always felt that my job allowed me to make a difference in the lives of people."

As a backcountry ranger, Bonnie spent many hours on horseback protecting the park environment by patrolling for poachers, checking fishing permits and creel, cleaning campsites, and clearing trails. Resource and wildlife protection has always been a very important part of her Park Service career. Her dog also provides assistance in tracking people who may not want to be found, such as poachers and antler hunters.

Bonnie says that, as a coroner, her job of protecting people extends to taking care of those who are no longer able to speak for themselves. "Determining the cause and manner of the death, being sure that the body has been properly cared for, and caring for the family is an important role of the coroner."

Now that she is retired from her position as a ranger in law enforcement, Bonnie is busier than ever working with Gator, who is certified in trailing, wilderness area searches, avalanche and water recovery, finding cadavers and human remains, and drug detection. She continues as a coroner for Gallatin County, and a trail ride on her horse, Twister, is never far from her thoughts.

Rescue: Bonnie and Gator near the west entrance to Yellowstone National Park, Wyoming.

"Growing up in Yellowstone was a tad different from growing up like a normal girl. We didn't have pets like cats and dogs. We had snakes."

Eleanor "Ellie" Hamilton Povah

Matriarch of the Hamilton family store tradition

Adventurous, spunky, hardworking, generous, and open-hearted—this is how people, including former employees of Hamilton Stores, describe Ellie. She says, "My life started off with plenty of adventures." Six years before her birth, her father purchased the lower store at Old Faithful and began a concession business that would span eighty-eight years and three generations. In 1920 her parents, Charles and May Hamilton, were the first civilian couple to be married at the historic Fort Yellowstone chapel in Mammoth Hot Springs. After Ellie's birth in 1921, the family spent summers in Yellowstone living in an apartment over the general store and winters in Santa Monica, California.

Life in Yellowstone can be dangerous. At the age of two and a half, Ellie managed to escape the watchful eyes of adults and fall into a scalding thermal pool. Treatment at the time consisted of immersion in olive oil baths, and she healed without a single scar.

She grew up making pets of garter snakes and learning to ride horses with Yellowstone wranglers who led visitors on trail rides. By the age of twelve she was greeting visitors at the lower Hamilton store soda fountain and taking their drink orders. At age fifteen she became the full-time manager of the soda fountain. Her comfort with snakes created opportunities for practical jokes on boys in the area. She especially liked hiding snakes in secret places for them to find.

During a winter back in Santa Monica, in 1939, Ellie met Trevor Povah and went on a horseback ride that led to a sixty-year marriage, four children, and continuation of life with the family business in Yellowstone. Ellie and Trevor began managing the day-to-day operations of the stores in 1948, but her father was still "in command" until he died in 1957. At one point in time, the Hamilton family owned all of the stores and gas stations in the park. After Trevor's death in 2001, Ellie continued to divide her life between Yellowstone and California, taking any opportunity to enjoy the outdoors—especially on horseback.

In addition to funding the Povah Community/Senior Center in West Yellowstone and supporting a new library in the old bank building, Ellie's generous legacy includes her donation of more than 1,100 Native American artifacts and Yellowstone memorabilia, including an authentic Yellowstone bus, to the Museum of the Rockies in Bozeman, Montana. Ellie and her family have made a unique and lasting contribution to Yellowstone history.

History: Ellie stands among artifacts collected by her family over eighty-eight years during the Hamilton Stores era in Yellowstone National Park.

"I've logged more than 250,000 miles on the Yellowstone roads on horseback, driving, or walking, visiting our stores."

Pat Povah

Member of Hamilton family stores tradition

New Year's Eve of 2002 was a sad day for Pat Povah and his family. It marked the end of eighty-eight years of a unique family business whose story is entwined with the entire history of Yellowstone National Park. In fact, the first Hamilton Store was acquired in 1915, predating the organization of the National Park Service in 1916.

Pat's grandfather, Charles Ashworth Hamilton, moved to Yellowstone in 1905 to take a summer job as an assistant to the purchasing agent for the Yellowstone Park Association at Mammoth Hot Springs. Ten years later, with a loan from a friend, Charles purchased the Klamer Store, built in 1896 at Old Faithful, for $20,000. He established his home in a six-room apartment above the store and pasted the two canceled checks he used to buy the store on the wall in a room used as his office. Each check issued by Hamilton Stores subsequently ended up on the wall until, on the day that Charles died in 1956, owning seventeen stores within the park, it had become the "million-dollar room," with the total value of checks exceeding $1.8 million.

Pat and his brother, Terry, were the third generation to manage and run Hamilton Stores, where goods have ranged from Native American artifacts traded for canned goods at the beginning of the twentieth century to animal hides, saddles, blankets, toothbrushes, and anything else that might have been forgotten by a traveler. "We had to have a little of everything," said Pat. "We were a true general store—food, clothing, souvenirs, local art, even furniture." The original store, at Old Faithful, still looks like a historic outpost with its welcoming knotty pine archway.

The Hamilton family was also noted as an excellent employer over the years, and many workers enjoyed a long tenure with the company. When the business changed hands on December 31, 2002, because of the bidding process required for concessions within the park, the staff included numerous people who had worked there for more than thirty years. Previously, two staff members had retired after forty-seven years of employment. "We tried to take good care of our employees and our customers," said Pat.

"Growing up in Yellowstone was an extraordinary experience," says Pat, "along with the opportunity to be part of such a family business and meet so many interesting people over the years."

Million-Dollar Room: Pat, holding a picture of his grandfather's original office, now being restored by the Yellowstone Park Foundation.

"Get out into the world and explore—and try making art! Just keep pushing the boundaries of what you know."

Mimi Matsuda

Former Yellowstone National Park interpretive ranger, naturalist, artist

The splendor of Yellowstone has inspired artistic expression for more than a century, from landscape painting to symphonies to magnificent photography, but few artists have melded their art with science, nature, and whimsy like Mimi Matsuda. In her studio you'll find four-foot-long trout on pine; velvety soft pastels of owls, herons, and bears; and a whimsical "secret lives" series, including an eagle rowing across Yellowstone Lake and a family of bison cross-country skiing.

About painting she says, "I always start my drawings with the eyes of the animal I am portraying. With the spotted owl, their deep and dark eyes captivate me."

It all started when she fell in love with national parks. The National Park Service and its interpretive rangers are glowing memories for Mimi when she recalls summertime vacations she took as a child with her parents. "It seemed like the most important kind of work," she says. "To teach about the wonders of the park."

After graduating from college with a degree in biology, she landed a position removing invasive nonnative trout from Yellowstone Lake in order to protect the endangered cutthroat trout. Next came nine years as a National Park Service ranger naturalist at Grand Teton and Yellowstone. At Fishing Bridge in Yellowstone, she enhanced her programs by developing illustrated posters and handouts for hikes and talks with visitors to better explain the wonders of the park.

Using her artwork to connect people with the natural environment led her to a new career as a full-time artist. Today she paints to encourage people to connect emotionally with nature, sometimes through the sheer beauty, sometimes with humor. She hopes these connections will lead to preservation and protection of wildlands and animals. "Every painting is an opportunity to tell a story."

When asked how her "Secret Lives of Animals" series evolved, Mimi says, "I've always loved science, sports, conservation, and the universality of humor. People can identify with the imagery and put themselves in the situation. It's a different kind of wildlife watching. They identify with the imagery and the animal. I hope it will help them want to care for this magical place."

Gone Fishing: Mimi fishes for "trout" in Yellowstone River, Livingston, Montana.

"I'm a Yellowstone person—for life!"

Dave Peterson

Photographer, Yellowstone resident artist, author

The beginning of Dave Peterson's story in Yellowstone is a familiar one: "I graduated from high school in Nebraska and got a job at the Lake Hotel for my first summer in Yellowstone."

Seventeen years passed and Dave had performed every job possible, from housekeeping to wait staff to employee dining room cook. The twist in his story, though, was that he had dedicated himself to learning photography during leisure moments and off-season, and by the late 1990s he had published his first book, *Yellowstone: Like No Other Place on Earth.* He hadn't quite arrived at the pinnacle of success, though. When a copy of his book sold in the hotel gift shop, Dave would have to leave his job cooking or serving in the dining room to provide an autograph. "I learned by doing. Animals were not interesting to me at first, but they became more of a focus as I started seeing a lot more of them."

Since those early years of "working like a hamster" to support his photography habit, Dave has published four more books and become Yellowstone's resident artist. Today he spends the summer season working in the lobby of Old Faithful Lodge, speaking with visitors as they crowd into his display of books, photographs, framed and unframed prints, and calendars. His photography is popular among visitors and collectors and has evolved from primarily landscapes to wildlife and even aerial work. He still spends every available moment with camera in hand, waiting for the opportunity to catch unusual photos.

"The backcountry thermal areas are a lot more interesting than the ones close to the roadside, but there are particular photos that I know people want to see because it is their idea of what Yellowstone is—like a bison standing near Old Faithful when it's erupting."

Perseverance throughout all working and weather conditions has been one of the keys to Dave's success. He doesn't cease to search for photography subjects throughout all seasons. In October you might find him camping in the Grand Teton National Park for a few weeks to catch the last brilliant lights and colors of fall. From there he may be headed to Thailand with his camera for a few months to capture a different experience of place before heading back to Yellowstone.

Photographer in the Mist: Dave studies his photography subjects from every angle.

"Yellowstone is a place where we are not controlling nature."

Timothy Townsend

Canyon District ranger at Canyon Village, Yellowstone National Park

Tim Townsend has no stories of family vacations to Yellowstone or being entranced by a cross-country adventure right after graduating from high school that brought him to the park. He grew up in Yellowstone after his father landed a job with the National Park Service in telecommunications in 1979 and moved the family to Mammoth Hot Springs. He has witnessed the dramatic effects of the forest fires of 1988, the reintroduction of wolves, and the battles against invasive plant and fish species, and says, "For the most part Yellowstone probably looks the same as it did 500 years ago. We might have had more predators and less prey in some years, but that's normal. Our goal is to have this place be the same in two hundred or a thousand"

As one of seven district supervisors for Yellowstone, he's in a good position to work toward that goal. He manages long-term strategies, overall operations, and budget planning for the Canyon District, located in the middle of Yellowstone. There, the ranger staff provides law enforcement, emergency services, resource education, and visitor assistance while managing wildlife jams and patrolling the trails and camping areas in the wild. Tim notes that the continued increase in visitation in recent years, along with the development of the gateway communities and population increases in the areas around Yellowstone, are all part of the big challenges to keeping Yellowstone wild while still responding to the public's healthy interest in the park.

"There's a big need for continued visitor education and monitoring of our visitors about wild animals and how to behave around them. While the park has seen many changes during its history, with more visitors and new and improved roads and infrastructure, lots of things haven't changed. When you watch a herd of bison grazing in Hayden Valley, they are doing the same thing they have always done on the same unchanged, wild landscape.

"I think the park has an equalizing effect on everyone. People from all walks of life and all corners of the globe are equally awed by an eruption of Old Faithful. Most employees have tears in their eyes when they leave the park for a new job."

For Tim, the park provides the right balance of people and solitude, and he gets "to see grizzlies, wolves, and geysers on [his] way to get groceries." He says he loves interacting with people, but in the winter he cherishes the simplicity and dead silence of the place. He wants visitors to connect with the national park idea: "We can leave nature to do what it does without cutting down trees or culling herds. We can allow fires to happen. We can let nature bring us into the future."

Home: Tim stands in his former elementary school classroom in Mammoth Hot Springs.

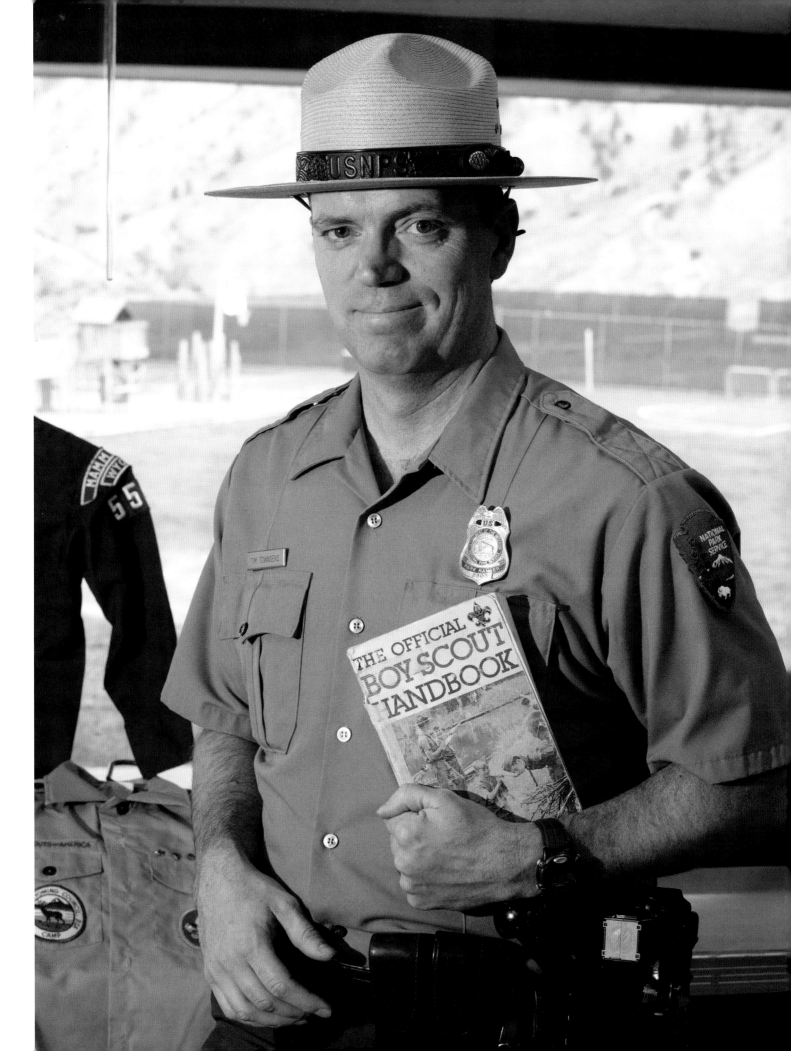

"My heritage goes back to the very beginnings of Yellowstone National Park."

Bob Coe

Innkeeper at historic Pahaska Tepee

William "Buffalo Bill" Cody was well known for his love of hunting and fishing, and he enjoyed nothing more than enticing friends to join him on western adventures, especially in the vicinity of Yellowstone. Bob Coe's grandfather was one of those fortunate friends and was encouraged by Buffalo Bill to buy a ranch in Cody, Wyoming, and bring the family out by rail each summer.

When Cody built Pahaska Tepee in 1905, designed by artist Abraham Archibald Anderson to accommodate tourists traveling up along the North Fork of the Shoshone River, no one could have guessed that eighty years later it would become the dream job of Bob Coe to run Pahaska Tepee as a resort and continue the family's long connection to the area.

Pahaska is nestled amongst the pines at the foot of Cody Peak and is the last private property before the east entrance to Yellowstone National Park. The main structure (the "Tepee") is a two-story log building about eighty-four by sixty feet facing east, toward the Shoshone River valley, with porches on the north, south, and east. Inside is a great stone fireplace. One can imagine the conversations of the guests back in 1905 from all over the country, describing their first encounters with wildlife as they dined on fresh-caught trout and wild mushrooms.

Bob had grown up with the dream of owning Pahaska and running it as a resort, and the property at last became available in 1984. Pahaska Tepee has been listed on the National Register of Historic Places. At one point, it was almost completely devastated by fire. It now operates as a mountain resort, with the original hunting lodge open for tours. Bob says that meeting visitors is very rewarding and he's always ready to suggest the best routes to the Dragon's Cauldron, the Grand Canyon of Yellowstone, and the Lamar Valley. "I always make sure that visitors know how to stay out of harm's way with animals. Wildlife is all around us here and we can't take them for granted. They're still wild even if they're roaming around in our backyard."

Bob also stays connected to his family history by serving on an advisory board for the Plains Indian tribe, overseeing curators who are working with a vast collection of Native American artifacts at the Buffalo Bill Museum of the West. He's thankful every day for his long and rewarding relationship with the people and the place.

Saving History: Bob and members of the Cody, Wyoming, community have battled to save historic buildings like Pahaska Tepee from physical deterioration and fire.

"I've done everything from the ground up as a carpenter."

Wayne Goutermont

Carpenter, hunting guide

As a boy growing up in the West, Wayne Goutermont learned a variety of skills over the years by working in jobs that involved building a variety of structures ranging from traditional log cabins to contemporary geodesic dome houses, to guiding hunters deep into forests, to working for the fire management office in Yellowstone. So he didn't hesitate when he became involved in the restoration of the Ordo Templi Orientalis—or OTO Homestead—also known as the oldest dude ranch in Montana. As Wayne describes it, "It was another thing that just happened!"

In fact, with his host of skills and practical knowledge of building, Wayne was a driving force in not only saving the ranch from destruction because of its advanced deterioration, but also organizing hundreds of volunteers who signed on to participate in rebuilding the ranch.

"Rebuilding the OTO was my favorite project, but also the most challenging. We had 1,800 volunteers over the years, and some of them were little old ladies who didn't know which end of a hammer was which. Sometimes we had to deal with big logs. It was a hoot, but we got it done."

The OTO (named for a religious order) was started by James Randall and his wife, Dora, in the late nineteenth century after they purchased squatters' rights on a small cabin with a dirt floor and a sod roof (now in the northwest corner of Yellowstone National Park). By 1912, Randall was courting wealthy eastern clients to come out West for an authentic western ranch experience. Theodore Roosevelt was one of the early guests. The ranch was upgraded over the years, eventually sold, and finally closed permanently in 1939. In 1991, in a severely deteriorated condition, it was donated to the U.S. Forest Service. Ten years later, Wayne and another builder set to work to preserve the historic structure. "There was no money, but a few of us decided to just do something on our own. Eventually we got enough done that the forest service saw what we were trying to do. Materials were donated and some funding was found—along with all those volunteers! We lured a cook and had all the meals right on the site."

Today Wayne says he is becoming very good at doing nothing in retirement as he travels with his wife around the country by RV. But he was proud to save a piece of western history. "I knew there was a good reason I'd learned how to do almost anything with a saw and a hammer."

Restored: Wayne at the historic OTO dude ranch near Gardiner, Montana.

"Yellowstone changed my relationship with music."

Martha Colby

Official Yellowstone National Park musician, cellist, and pianist

Martha Colby wears the most unusual uniform of anyone who works at Yellowstone. Guests at the Old Faithful Inn can find her five nights a week, dressed in black evening attire, playing either her cello or the piano. Her unique musical background—growing up listening to all types of music, along with her rigorous musical training at the Carolina School for the Arts and the Berklee College of Music in Boston—prepared her for the rare opportunity to become Yellowstone's official musician.

She started piano lessons at age four with a family member and then switched to the cello in fourth grade. When she went on to music school, she had to choose one instrument. "It was a difficult choice," she says about giving up her beloved piano. After playing for many years as a cellist in many ensembles, a friend asked her in 2007 to fill in with a group playing at the Old Faithful Inn for a brief stint, and she jumped at the chance. She had visited once before and was already hooked on Yellowstone's beauty and serenity.

Back in 1989, driving across the country with a friend, she had spent one night in Yellowstone, and her memories of waterfalls and green forests reviving after the extensive forest fires of 1988 had stayed with her. Best of all, when her temporary cellist job came to an end, she was hired as a pianist!

"It was serendipity," she says. "The ancient wisdom of this magical place knew that I was really a pianist who happened to play the cello, and now I can do both!"

Martha plays all styles of music. "I love it all," she says. "Dixie, jazz, Broadway, blues, classical."

When not performing or practicing she backpacks, hikes, or enjoys life with her 150 coworkers who staff the park during the winter months, participating in blind skiing, or a tug-of-war on skis, or the bison chip toss during staff Olympics. She's especially drawn to the area around Thumper, the black sand pool that started thumping and bubbling in 2011. "You can hold on to the fence around the pool and feel the ground tremble."

In the summer months, she loves performing at Lake Yellowstone Hotel, where she meditates by the lake every morning. When asked where her music might carry her next, she says she'll stay put as long as she can.

"This place keeps you young! My predecessor retired at eighty-three. I've got lots of time and lots of music left to play."

Timeless: Martha performs her original music compositions in the historic Old Faithful Inn.

"My ultimate goal is that when visitors leave the park, they leave with the idea that we all live on this one planet together and we're all connected."

Harlan Kredit

Yellowstone National Park ranger, award-winning science teacher

For more than forty years, Harlan Kredit has finished each year as a high school science teacher in Lynden, Washington; packed up his family; and headed to Yellowstone, where he spends his summers as a ranger naturalist. In addition to serving on the Yellowstone Fire Department for thirty-five years and as a National Park Service photographer in the past, he is also trained in emergency medicine and teaches environmental education to teachers at the American Wilderness Leadership School in Jackson, Wyoming.

Visitors to Fishing Bridge in Yellowstone soon realize that they are in the presence of a dedicated and inspired teacher who believes that people learn when they are given higher levels of responsibility. "I want to wake up their basic curiosity about the world. They should be asking: 'Why, why, why?' They need to use their five senses."

There is a lot of evidence that Harlan's teaching approach is working. He has been recognized with over twenty-five awards and honors, including the Presidential Award for Excellence in Mathematics and Science Teaching and the National Conservation Teacher of the Year in 2004, and he has been inducted into the National Teachers Hall of Fame.

Growing up in Puget Sound watching salmon activity, he realized as early as 1974 that the fish population was in serious danger. His first class project as a science teacher involved hatching 5,000 salmon eggs using a pump, a kiddie pool, and a fiberglass box the students made in shop. Today, still working in that original stream, the kids raised more than 50,000 Coho salmon and have planted more than 18,000 trees. "My senior biology class is in charge of the hatchery; my sophomores do the riparian-zone work, like planting trees. Field trips are designated "slightly grubby," "medium grubby," and "maximum grubby." Sophomores might be teaching fourth-graders to plant trees in a downpour. If you want kids to invest in something, empower them to do it."

His goal as a Yellowstone interpretive ranger has been to talk with people about the importance of protecting the park and to explain the complex biological connections that are fundamental to preservation. He suggests that visitors "read the landscape, walk down the trail, look around you, and tell what you see. Close your eyes. Listen and smell." His favorite place is the top of Avalanche Peak. "You have to work hard to get there, but you can see the same vast landscape that the Native Americans saw."

Master Teacher: Harlan has won many awards for his unique methods of science teaching.

"I never let Yellowstone be too far away."

Bill Chapman

Artist, wrangler, fire guard, pilot

Few people have a connection to Yellowstone that is as unique and long as Bill Chapman. His father was a permanent park ranger, working all seasons of the year, and Bill "arrived" by dogsled in 1930 to Bechler Park Station, where the family was stationed. According to Bill, storks don't work in the winter in Yellowstone.

His preschool years were spent at park ranger stations, completely isolated during the winter except for "old park people." He was not at a loss for playmates, though. Animals, and the old-timers with their yarns about the old days, were his favorite companions.

By age fourteen, in 1944, Bill was a wrangler and ranch hand at Yellowstone Trails Ranch near the north entrance. During the school year he was "boarded out" in Bozeman, Montana, so that he could attend high school. Summers were spent wrangling at ranches throughout the area until he was old enough, in 1949, to live alone at the Pelican patrol cabin, where he worked as a fire guard and packed in supplies to the Pelican Cone Lookout.

After college, a stint in the army, and learning to fly airplanes, he flew telemetry research flights for the park, tracked radio-collared animals, conducted game counts, searched for lost hikers, and mapped forest fires. As a certified flight instructor, he taught several Yellowstone rangers how to fly.

Through it all, however, Bill was drawing and painting. His father was also an accomplished artist, and the family made good use of those many seasons of isolation in the park, passing on their love of art to Bill, who became a designer of interpretive exhibits for the Yellowstone Library and Museum Association. Eventually he contracted with Yellowstone and several other national parks to construct and paint roadside and museum exhibits.

Long winters without playmates in his early years also gave Bill time for reading. All those solitary years of observation, listening to stories, and watching wildlife melded with Bill's love for comic books. "Creating the comic book version of *Yarns of the Yellowstone* had always been my dream."

As he looks out today from his home over the huge span of Yellowstone's Northern Range and watches herds of buffalo across the river in the park, he is thankful for his lifelong relationship with Yellowstone through long, quiet winters to bright summer skies.

Comic Book Kid: Bill has combined his vast knowledge of Yellowstone, his artistic skills, and his sense of humor to teach kids about the park through comics.

"In Yellowstone you need to be a constant learner. You can never learn all there is to know."

Julianne Baker

Naturalist, educator, former National Park Service ranger

At sunrise the sound of an elk bugle can be heard through the dense forest. Later in the day, ducks and geese are seen coasting across the ponds of Hayden Valley. Coyotes, otters, mink, and red squirrels are spotted in various locations. A group of six hikers, armed with notebooks, have scribbled notes throughout the day about the sights, sounds, and smells they've encountered.

As the hikers take off their backpacks and settle down for the evening, Julianne Baker, who teaches guides how to guide, checks in with each member of the group to see how they are: "Any sore or red spots on your feet? We want to prevent blisters before they happen. Tomorrow we will be covering about seven miles."

Julianne, the first resident instructor of the Yellowstone Association, (now Yellowstone forever), loves these opportunities to take a group of naturalists-in-training into the backcountry of Yellowstone, where they spend days observing and recording whatever plants and wildlife they may encounter. With a master's degree in outdoor environmental education and Wilderness First Responder training, she is prepared for her position. But she also has wisdom from experience.

"In the wild, you must continually evaluate the risk of each action. Is it high risk with low consequences—perhaps fording a stream by walking across on slippery rocks? Or is it high risk with high consequences—like crossing a river on a tree branch, twenty feet above the water? My students are learning how to make decisions for themselves and evaluate the decisions of people they will eventually be guiding."

Julianne teaches people ages twenty-one to seventy whose experience ranges from those who have hiked many backcountry trails to those who have never camped before. Besides making sure they have the right supplies (and attitude!), she appraises their stamina and tolerance for strenuous hiking. All students record their observations using the Grinnell method, in which, at the end of each day, the students transform their scattered notes into a narrative accompanied by pictures, maps, and drawings. At some point in the training, each participant must lead an hourlong hike with the instructor and demonstrate both an ability to work with people and an understanding of the place and the natural environment.

For Julianne, working as a guide's guide in Yellowstone is the culmination of a lifetime spent teaching others and enjoying nature, and that experience has brought her to the center of where she needs to be: understanding nature with people.

Be Prepared: Fallen trees can be dangerous. Julianne teaches her students skills for all levels of challenges in the wild.

"For a combat-wounded veteran, being out in the wild, fishing, hunting, and communicating with other wounded vets is great medicine."

Brett Miller

Founder and director of Warfighters Outfitters, combat veteran

"Can't do it" is not a phrase in Brett Miller's vocabulary. After a roadside bomb in Iraq in 2004 left him with a traumatic brain injury, a detached right retina, nine fractured teeth, and paralysis on his left side, he spent three years in a hospital and two years in rehabilitation thinking about what he could do. And he started on the long road back to a new normal. Through the Wounded Warrior Project he became a champion cycler and completed a 3,000-mile race from Oceanside, California, to Annapolis, Maryland. He says: "The Wounded Warrior Project renewed my courage and enabled me to do things that I would never have been able to do on my own."

What followed combined his love for fishing and hunting with his concept of what could be healing and therapeutic for other wounded veterans. Today, Brett's nonprofit, completely free guide service, Warfighters Outfitters, is tailored to meet the needs of veterans regardless of their medical limitations. "If you can get here, we can get you in the water or in the woods."

Besides fishing and hunting expeditions, each year Warfighters Outfitters also hosts an "engagement" event in Yellowstone during which a group of ten to twenty participants rebuild a structure or a corral. Nights are spent in a nearby hotel rather than outside to accommodate needs of amputees and those requiring electricity for medical treatments and refrigerated medication. Brett says that these rebuilding projects are hugely gratifying, especially for veterans who fought unpopular wars.

"They've come together and created something they're proud of and can show their grandchildren."

Brett feels that fishing, hunting, and building structures outdoors is restorative because the mind is engaged, the air is clean, and motivation and esprit de corps are strong. "They're not thinking about their stress. There's a lot of smiling, and at some point in the week, the stories come."

People are invited back the next year if they can bring a comrade who needs the experience more than they do, especially those who are in need but haven't been the recipient of beneficial events like this. Brett says that this project is also an important part of his own continuing recovery. "I'm reminded every day that I have nothing to complain about, that there are people who are much worse off than me, and we can do this together."

Courageous: Brett relaxes in the midst of rebuilding a corral during an engagement project for wounded veterans in Yellowstone National Park.

"Yellowstone is the best place in the world to view wolves in their natural habitat."

Rick McIntyre

Biological technician for the Yellowstone wolf project

It's 4:00 A.M. in Slough Creek and Rick McIntyre, telemeter in hand, has already located a signal from a wolf pack with a radio-collared member. The next step will be to get close enough with his spotting scope to observe and carefully note their activities and behaviors. When he has located a pack, Rick says he still feels the same excitement and sense of thrill as he did on his first sighting back in 1996—and he has never taken a "sick" day. Missing a day of wolf watching is not an option.

"I might miss something important. It would be like missing your kid's first music recital. You never know what you might see."

Rick is observing and recording the lives of individual wolves who are among the succeeding generations of the first packs to be reintroduced to the park in the Yellowstone Gray Wolf Restoration Project.

Accompanying Rick on his daily regimen is thrilling for visitors, but these excursions are also an important way to make people aware of the importance of wolves in the Yellowstone ecosystem. "It's rewarding to share my knowledge with a visitor and see their excitement when they first see a wolf. Some wolves have become famous among wolf watchers and it's kind of like spotting a movie star."

Rick says that visitors are always impressed when they observe the civility of wolves toward each other, especially when a pack of wolves are eating a carcass together. Until recently, much of our general information about wolves in popular culture was based on documentaries of captive wolves, who tend to be more aggressive and competitive for food than those who live in a wild pack. Observers are also surprised by the quiet confidence of male wolves. Leadership of the ranking male in a pack is not forced and does not seem to be experienced as domineering by those in his group.

After more than twenty years of observation, Rick has gained a perspective on female leadership in wolf packs. Females seem to do most of the decision making, including where to travel and when to hunt and rest.

For Rick, every new tidbit of information that he can add to the growing body of knowledge about wolf behavior is nourishing, both personally and professionally. He is content to spend every moment of daylight waiting and watching, so he can be there for those fantastic "Eureka!" moments.

Wolf Watcher: Rick equipped to spot and observe wolves in the wild.

"When you are in bear country, you know you're in a special place."

Louisa Willcox

Conservationist, grizzly bear advocate, mountaineer

Grizzly bears have many strengths, including high intelligence, an excellent ability to remember, and a keen sense of smell that enables them to detect food from great distances. They are good swimmers and fast runners, reaching speeds as high as 35 mph over land. They give birth during hibernation and are very protective of their cubs for two to three years. Grizzlies are selective about the plants they eat and can doctor themselves by eating dirt to clean out their system and replace their potassium. They can till glacier lilies like farmers, dig for roots, and transform the ecosystem around them. Native Americans who lived alongside grizzly bears described them in stories as "uncles," healers, mentors and guides, symbols of transformation and resurrection. But today, the future of the grizzly is in question.

Louisa Willcox has fought for the survival of grizzlies for three decades, first with the Greater Yellowstone Coalition, then with the Sierra Club, and most recently as senior wildlife advocate at the Natural Resources Defense Council. Her first encounter with a bear when she was a seventeen-year-old mountaineering instructor opened her mind to the spiritual connection between Native Americans and grizzlies.

"I was coming down off a ridge as it was getting dark, looking for a space to camp, and I literally bumped into a grizzly bear. In that instant, the animal transformed the space. We looked at each other, and I felt in the presence of wildness and profound intelligence. The bear walked away. Bears do the right thing, just about always."

At one time grizzlies could be found from Mexico to Alaska, but today their wilderness habitat in the lower forty-eight states has diminished to six island ecosystems, with the stongholds centered on Glacier and Yellowstone National Parks. This represents less than 2 percent of the area occupied by bears when Europeans first arrived on the continent. If endangered-species protections were removed (or delisted), the Yellowstone grizzly's survival would be uncertain. As the battle for their protection is fought in courts and public opinion, Louisa observes that it has now become a spiritual argument. Forty-one Native American tribes have requested a moratorium on delisting until the government has consulted with them about their spirtual and cultural concerns.

"No one is neutral about grizzly bears. Native Americans want to guard their legacy as ancestors. Local governments see them as an impediment to progress because they prey on livestock. It is a war of symbols."

For Louisa, protecting the grizzly bear is part of advocating for effective conservation methods as well as supporting the preservation of our important relationship as humans with wildness.

"While there are many examples of successful efforts to coexist with bears, there is little systematic analysis of what worked where and why—but they must survive."

Advocate: Louisa believes that the grizzly bear still exists because people care.

"Yellowstone grabbed my heart back in 1974."

Bob Berry

Author, collector of Yellowstone memorabilia

Back in 1847, before computers, TV, film, and record players, an enterprising photographer came up with an idea to provide sensational home entertainment in the form of a cardboard card with two seemingly identical images, side by side. When viewed through a stereoscope, the image jumped into action in lifelike 3-D. Suddenly people were able to view a picture of a scene—like Old Faithful, Niagara Falls, a barnyard, or a first kiss—with surprising and scintillating realism, as if they were actually viewing the image in real life. Hundreds of thousands of stereo view cards were produced by several companies between 1850 and 1952, until the medium was replaced by realist-format 3-D slide viewers and the View-Master.

Bob Berry remembers a stereoscope and stereo view cards in the library of his elementary school in the 1950s. They might have provided his first realistic impression of Egypt or Africa, but his enduring romance with the medium did not begin until the 1980s when a collector friend in Texas reintroduced him to the medium at a regional meeting of the National Stereographic Association.

"I had traveled back to Yellowstone at every opportunity ever since I traveled through it in 1974, and here, at this meeting, were fabulous 3-D views of the place."

He bought a box of stereo view cards, and the rest is history. Bob was soon collecting not only stereo views and stereo view equipment but any bits of history and memorabilia about Yellowstone that he could find. Today he has the largest privately held collection of historic photography, primarily stereo views, related to Yellowstone in the world. Ken Burns used Bob's collection during the filming of his documentaries about the national park system and the life of Theodore Roosevelt.

What is the daily life of an avid collector? Bob and his wife support his passion for collecting by operating a bed-and-breakfast, the Robin's Nest, in Cody, Wyoming, where he might be found serving "Bob's Upside Down Cream Cheese Stuffed Praline Toast." He has also coauthored *Yellowstone Yesterday & Today,* illustrated with his stereo views of the park, but most days he can be found at his computer, trawling for that rare view of the Old Faithful Inn under construction or a group of tourists who had been released after being held as prisoners by the Nez Perce tribe in the nineteenth century.

"It's fun and exhilarating and I'm constantly looking at images of a place I love."

Enjoying the View: Bob holds some of his more than 4,200 stereo view cards depicting Yellowstone.

"Almost fifty years of watching bears has not quelled my curiosity about the great bruins."

Jim Halfpenny

Naturalist, scientist, educator, author, animal tracker

On a sunny September day, stepping into the classroom of Jim Halfpenny's A Naturalist's World in Gardiner, Montana, one can feel the presence of many others who have left "impressions" on Jim: plaster-cast prints of bears, elk, bison, wolves, and many other wild inhabitants of Yellowstone and the world lie on tables and shelves. Even Bigfoot is represented.

Students of animal tracking and behavior come from all over the world to attend the classes Jim teaches for the Smithsonian Institute and other organizations. They learn the skills needed to go out into the wild and see wild animals—or at least to recognize which animals are in the area. Jim teaches about and observes wildlife all over the world, from pole to pole, but says, "Yellowstone is still the place to go to see animals."

His students range in age from eight to eighty, but everyone must be ready to get "down and dirty" in the fieldwork portion of the class, as they learn to decipher old and new bear markings on trees, and the age and condition of scat (animal droppings), and to make casts of footprints found on the trail. While Jim's courses are focused on ecology, he says that the first thing people want to see is bear and wolf tracks. "They can't talk about ecology until they see that."

Since 1961 Jim has taught outdoor education and environmental programs for state, federal, and private organizations, including Yellowstone, and is the author of many books. His home base near the north entrance to the park has facilitated his knowledge of generations of wolves, bears, and other animals. Those who are fortunate enough to take a class with Jim will not only come away with a detailed knowledge of animals and ecology, but may also have an opportunity to visit Bear Valley, a secret location in Yellowstone where, as Jim describes, "Walking along its narrow bottom, you can feel the presence of grizzlies and black bears, and at the upper end of the valley sits an art gallery of bear claw marks etched into the white bark of aspens."

During decades of watching and studying animals and participating in scientific studies and exchange of information, Jim has also kept up with the development of digital technology. "The advantage of apps is especially helpful to navigation and interpretation, but in my classes we work with the real thing—the scat, the footprints, the bones. Come and join us. You'll see."

Evidence: Jim Halfpenny with his extensive collection of animal tracks and other artifacts in Gardiner, Montana.

"When you visit Yellowstone, get out of the car and away from the road. Try to be still and notice small things."

Karen Reinhart

Museum registrar, naturalist, author

Raising children in and around Yellowstone National Park could be a challenge for a parent from an urban environment, the suburbs, or even forested areas, but for Karen Wildung Reinhart, daughter of homesteaders in central Montana, it's been like raising them in paradise. Living with bears and animals of all kinds in the midst of beautiful country has given her children unmatched knowledge and values, she says.

Karen raised her family in the interior of the park, living at Lake station year-round for six years. Her three children hiked, skied, and explored nature throughout their childhoods. "They value being outside. They understand the habitats and space that animals need, and they're passionate about keeping things pristine."

Identifying plants, trees, and shrubs—and living in close proximity to bears and other animals that now occasionally pillage her gardens and orchards—are all part of the experience. "We try to harvest fruit and vegetables before the bears think they're perfect. They like carrots but not beets." On some days, ten to twenty deer or an elk herd can be seen gathered in her yard near Gardiner, Montana, just outside the northern boundary of the park next to the Yellowstone River.

Karen's love for the outdoors and wild places has also shaped her career. After college at Montana State University in Bozeman, she became an interpretive park ranger at Fishing Bridge in Yellowstone National Park. Karen led hikes and gave programs during the summer for fifteen years, educating visitors about park resources. Finally, she moved into her current position at Yellowstone Gateway Museum, where she manages collections and shares the stories of Yellowstone and its environs through curated exhibits of the museum's artifacts. Her skills as a naturalist and teacher are complemented by her eloquence of expression. In beautiful prose, accompanied by magnificent photographs, her book *Old Faithful Inn: Crown Jewel of National Park Lodges,* coauthored with Jeff Henry, recounts the history and charm of Yellowstone's oldest and most iconic lodge. She has also written about the extensive 1988 forest fires in *Yellowstone's Rebirth by Fire.*

Living on the border of Yellowstone, surrounded by nature in all aspects of daily life with her family, has "created an opportunity to make conscious decisions. We think about how we live in connection with wildness every day in this fantastic place."

The Bear Facts: Karen and daughter Emma in their backyard near Gardiner, Montana, examining the destructive results of apple picking by grizzly bears despite the family's efforts at picking up any fallen fruit.

"Nothing compares to Yellowstone in winter. It's the best of the best, especially while driving a snow coach."

Steve Blakeley

Transportation dispatcher at Yellowstone National Park

A frequent question about travel within Yellowstone's road system is: "Do I need a car?" Cars are definitely helpful for getting into the park, but, depending on where visitors stay, once arrived they can use Yellowstone's well-organized bus transportation system, complete with informed tour guides. The tradition of providing park vehicles and guides harkens back to the beginning of the twentieth century, when visitors arrived by train outside of the park and then were transported by stagecoach from the depot for delivery to the Old Faithful Inn. People traveled within the park mostly by coach and horseback until the 1930s, when hundreds of buses were purchased, most of which were usurped by a flood of cars after World War II.

Steve Blakeley was a student bus driver at Kent State University in 1977 when he was recruited to spend the summer driving a tour bus within Yellowstone. "Most of the drivers before that had worked for bus companies like Greyhound. The park was looking for younger seasonal employees."

He was hooked on Yellowstone after that first stint, returning for ten summers and working as a bellhop and bell captain at the Lake Yellowstone Hotel. He eventually became location manager at the Old Faithful Inn, the Lake Hotel, and the Snow Lodge.

He also had the opportunity to drive the classic Bombardier snow coaches in the winter, with their exhilarating ride close to the ground. Today, as dispatcher in the transportation system for Yellowstone's twenty-five vehicles and tour guides, he has a unique knowledge of the history of the vehicles used in Yellowstone.

"Hundreds of buses were sold off all over the country over the years. Some buses from the 1930s were bought by a guy in Skagway, Alaska, to meet cruise ships at the dock and drive people around town. They became a big piece of Alaska tourism."

In recent years, eight of the early Yellowstone buses have been bought back and restored. But Steve regrets that the old Bombardier snow coaches made in Quebec and brought to Yellowstone in 1955 will soon be phased out. In his opinion, "These old tracked 'bombs' are the best touring vehicles in Yellowstone."

When he has the chance to get away from the transportation department, Steve is an avid fan of disc golf and takes pride in the George Anderson course created at the Lake Yellowstone Hotel.

Life is good in Yellowstone, he says: "I'm a lucky guy."

Travels in the Past: Steve with a restored 1930s Yellowstone bus.

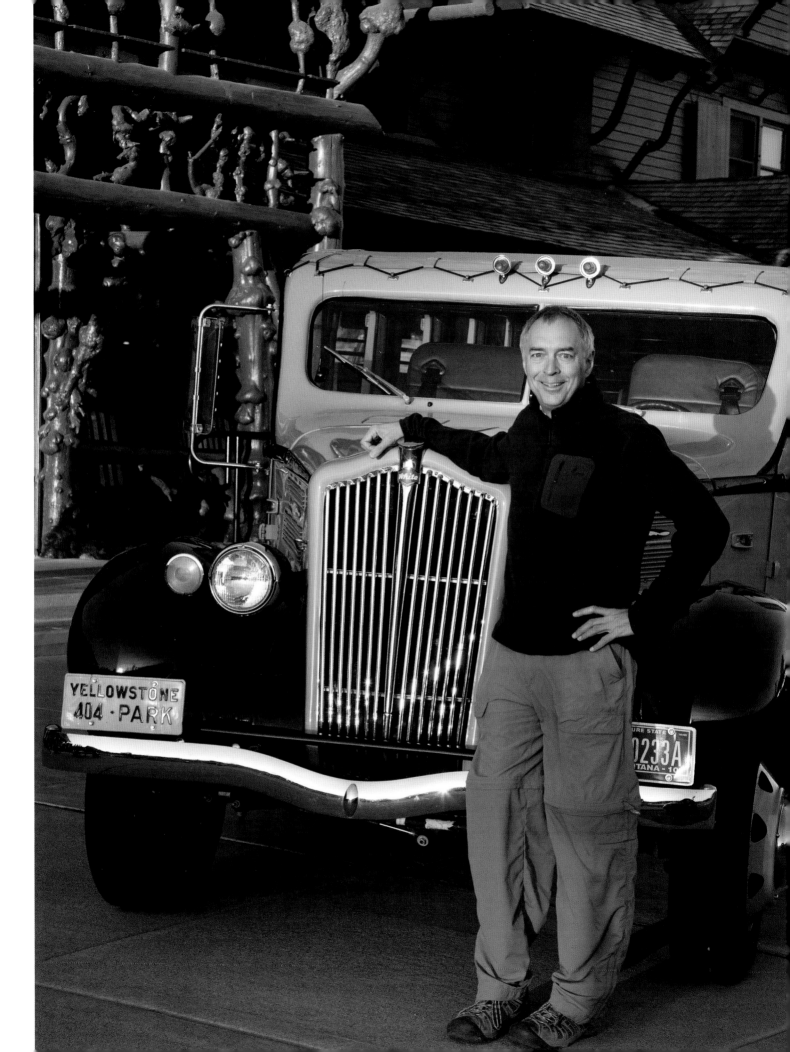

"Almost anything can happen in Yellowstone."

Max Brenzel

Auto mechanic, EMT, hiker

Imagine a place of about 3,500 square miles, about the size of Connecticut and Rhode Island combined, with five entrances, one on each side and two on the bottom, which all converge eventually into a single two-lane road traveled by millions of visitors each year, mainly in the summer months, in cars, buses, small trucks, and RVs. This is the automotive world of Yellowstone National Park. Traveling through the park on a good day without animal jams (when bison, elk, or deer are crossing the road and people must stop, or want to stop take pictures) may take four to five hours by car—which is plenty of time for almost anything to break, seize up, or boil over, especially at an altitude far above sea level. Needless to say, it is a difficult situation for both cars and people.

The good news is that Max Brenzel, an expert and seasoned auto mechanic, is there as well, along with other resourceful mechanics who work in service stations located in Old Faithful, Canyon, Fishing Bridge, and Gardiner. Max also answers as many as a hundred emergency calls each year as an EMT (emergency medical technician). "Yellowstone is a place where almost anything can happen," he says. "We had a guy run off the road recently and luckily was able to crawl out of the bushes. We had to find and fix both him and the car."

Max describes catching the "Yellowstone fever" when he came to work in the park in 1981. He loved both the place and the people and has run the repair shop at Canyon, worked in the marina at the lake, and delivered auto supplies to stations throughout the park. He says the repair shop at Fishing Bridge is the busiest. They work on the park's rescue vehicles as well as those of visitors. Car trouble in Yellowstone requires patience; waiting for a part for a broken RV can take up to two weeks, so the owners have no choice but to relax in the campground near the station.

During winter at the Snow Lodge in the past, Max changed tracks on snow coaches and worked on visitor's vehicles. Today he is focused on maintaining the Yellowstone fleet of three hundred cars, trucks, vans, snowmobiles, and snow coaches.

Max also loves hiking. He says that the mysteries of the mountains are more revealed in winter, but he is always ready to explore the trails in all seasons.

"Yellowstone is a land of beauty—and friendship. There's no place like it in the world," he says.

Mr. Fix-it: Max working in the service station for the Yellowstone vehicle fleet.

"One of the highlights of my job is to carry out a successful rescue operation."

Wendy Hafer

Helicopter operations specialist for Fire and Rescue

Yellowstone is a predictable destination for college graduates with degrees in fish and wildlife studies, and Wendy was no exception. She was fortunate to land her first position through the Student Conservation Association, tracking the movements of a pronghorn sheep herd.

After a series of seasonal jobs, she eventually found herself communicating via radio with Yellowstone first responders, initially ordering supplies and ultimately zooming up to the fast-paced role of dispatching: telling firefighters and rescue personnel in helicopters where they need to go.

She now supports the ranger division by managing the helicopter contract in Yellowstone National Park and supervising eight helitack pilots and crew, and she also oversees the firefighters who travel throughout the western United States. Wendy says that her job is very much behind the scenes, in spite of the sensational aspects of what she does.

"The public doesn't see me that often, but I know what they're doing. We're there when they need us."

Wendy says she is most proud of the young workers she has mentored over the years. "It's great to feel that they had a rewarding experience in firefighting and search-and-rescue and to see them moving on to even greater things."

Among the many significant and poignant moments in her career, she has overseen rescues from Granite Peak, the highest point in Montana, and searched for the son of a colleague and ranger who died in the Yellowstone River. Wendy says that when rescues become body recovery operations, it is a different kind of opportunity to assist the victim's family and loved ones by at least returning the body. She feels blessed every day to be able to get up and go to a job in which she takes pride in both her work and her colleagues. Her personal experiences of loss have made her acutely aware of the support of her Park Service "family."

"People band together and support each other through thick and thin in the park. I can't imagine working in another job and being without these folks."

There is one place besides Yellowstone that Wendy says she can imagine for herself and her two children, but it has its similarities to the park. "Someday I'd like to have a big, big ranch with livestock. I'm looking forward to watching out for a lot of animals."

Ready: Wendy holding an axe in front of a helicopter. The dispatcher's primary job is communicating during fire support and search-and-rescue operations.

"Yellowstone has so many trails to hike. It's such a pleasure to work and play here."

Molly Nelson

Civil engineer

Yellowstone National Park became the world's first national park on March 1, 1872, only 10 years after the Homestead Act had been passed, opening what remained of public land to private ownership and settlement. If Yellowstone had not been established and set aside to preserve its wildness, it would be a very different place today, blighted with businesses, private homes, and industry.

Almost 150 years later, Molly Nelson continues the call for stewardship of the area by working as an engineer in the park and promoting sustainable and renewable energy sources, water conservation, and utility projects in relation to the park's use as a recreation destination. Roadways, water supplies, bridges, power sources, and buildings within the park all must be maintained while keeping in mind resource protection and public opinion.

Molly's first park experience was working in a cafeteria for a concessionaire, serving food, disposing of food scraps, and washing dishes. What she learned in that position she considers to be valuable inside information, a part of the story about the park and how it is used that only someone who has worked there truly understands. Later, during her studies as an undergraduate engineering student, she returned to the park and gained a much different perspective as an intern working on a sustainability project that focused on irrigation in Mammoth Hot Springs. She now has a broad view of the life cycle of dishwashing water in the park.

These days she is back working in Yellowstone National Park as she completes her master's degree in civil engineering at Montana State University in Bozeman. "Life doesn't slow down in the park. Summer is construction season for projects and winter is planning and grant-writing time, and we're continually having to think about the impact of everything."

While her job does not afford much time for recreation, she has managed to enjoy some great hikes. She likes the Bechler region in the southwest, the lake area, and the old-growth forests that stretch through the Lamar Valley toward Cooke City. Her advice to visitors is to come in the shoulder seasons, especially the fall. "Yellowstone is gorgeous in September and October and the roads are a lot less crowded."

Sustainable: Molly monitors an irrigation project in Mammoth Hot Springs.

"I have known some wild animals for their entire lives."

George Bumann

Sculptor, naturalist, wildlife ecologist, teacher

For a sculptor who holds both bachelor's and master's degrees in wildlife ecology, George Bumann was not concerned when, during a busy day of sculpting outdoors in Mammoth Hot Springs inside Yellowstone National Park, three adult elk strolled by and stopped to inspect his creation. Two of the wild animals continued on, but the third licked the depiction of an elk and then started eating it. "This is just part of working out in the wild," said George. "You run the risk of your subject matter destroying what you've created."

George calls the Yellowstone environs his "big studio," and he is endlessly thankful for the opportunity to bring art and nature together every day. During his years working for the Yellowstone Association and fashioning representations of the animals he sees in the park, he has followed entire bloodlines, recognizing, for example, generations of wolves by their particular markings. He sculpted the matriarch of one of the early wolf packs reintroduced to the park—and her children and grandchildren. When a granddaughter of the original alpha pack strayed outside the park boundaries and was killed recently, George was comforted only by the fact that he had sculpted her and had known her on a much deeper level than most people experience wild animals.

He grew up in his mother's sculpture studio and in close proximity to the Oliver Stevens Blockhouse Museum, a cultural history museum created by his grandfather in upstate New York. George loved the atmosphere and environment of these two worlds and eventually came to realize that he could blend them together in his art.

"The subject itself is different from the subject matter. When I'm creating a sculpture of a bear, I'm making a human connection with something outside of myself. I realize that the more I try to understand something, like an animal, by creating it, the less I really know. What is the bear thinking? We humans in the Western world don't live enough with the elements and wild animals to know things in a natural way. We are strikingly separate from the natural world."

George's art, which reflects his deep desire to know and understand nature, can be found in exhibitions, private collections, and galleries around the world. But visitors to Yellowstone will likely find George outside next to a river or hot spring, working on a sculpture of a bull elk he's known for years and happy to stop and show visiting children how to find shapes and angles in the things they see around them and how to fashion a bird from clay.

"Describing nature with words is limited," he says. "Sculpture gives it another dimension of understanding."

Art and Nature: George holds a sculpture almost devoured by his subject.

"You don't get into a Piper Super Cub; you put it on."

Roger Stradley

Bush pilot, wildlife spotter and tracker

After sixty years of flying above Yellowstone, the wild blue yonder has a special meaning for Roger Stradley. He is considered one of the best bush pilots in the United States and has memorized the terrain within a 300-mile radius of Gallatin Field in Bozeman. He is able to count large herds of animals from an airplane flying at 80 miles per hour and can even distinguish between the males, females, and youngsters in the herd.

Flying is a family tradition. Roger's father, Jim Stradley, conducted the first aerial wildlife surveys counting elk and bison herds inside the park in the late 1940s. Roger and his brother Dave started flying by the age of seven with their father, and Roger accumulated 500 hours of flight time with his father before his first solo. Today, he has logged an incredible 63,000 hours of flying time.

His work with the wolf restoration project as one of the original pilots who monitored the wolves after their reintroduction in 1995 was crucial to the success of the program. Doug Smith, program leader, says that Roger is one of the few pilots with the necessary flying skill and knowledge of the terrain and the animals. Roger says that he can track anything that "walks, flies, or swims."

Doug and Roger have spent many hours flying above the park looking for wolves. Doug says that Roger is able to feel the air; he works with it rather than against it. The plane circles quietly enough above the animals so that it does not disturb them and they can be observed and counted in their natural state.

For Roger, there is no place he would rather be than flying over Yellowstone, pointing out wolves, grizzlies, elk, cougars, and eagles to whoever might be sitting behind him in his tiny yellow Cub. Roger counts every other type of wildlife as well, including birds, fish, beaver, wolverines, and pronghorn, and provides critical information to wildlife biologists. Roger describes Yellowstone as still wild: "You can fly all day and never see another person."

As he sits in his hangar on a foggy morning at 6:30, waiting for the sky to clear, he says, "Every day is another chance to fly above this magnificent park. I'll do it for as long as I can."

Airborne: Roger spots and tracks wildlife for a variety of agencies and biologists.

"I knew I wanted to be both in the wild and with people. Law enforcement was a dream job for me."

Colette Daigle-Berg

Member of Western Montana Search Dogs, Yellowstone National Park law enforcement ranger (retired)

From a distance, she looks like just another enthusiastic pet owner out for a romp in the snow with her dog, but then things get more curious: The dog disappears and Colette retreats into a large snow cave. This is high-stakes training time for her current search dog, Chapter, who knows there will be no rewards unless she can sniff her way back to Colette through several feet of snow.

Mandatory retirement at age fifty-seven was tough after thirty years as a law enforcement park ranger, but it opened up a new world for Colette. Today, she has entered a new "chapter" of her life, combining all of her forensic, investigatory, and people skills with her physical stamina and her love of dogs. She now responds to search-and-rescue operations all over the region as a member of Western Montana Search Dogs. "Leaving Yellowstone after retirement was not an option. I love living along the Yellowstone River," she says. "Search-and-rescue is perfect for me."

Search-and-rescue operations, which were only a small part of her former job, are intense and time-consuming and can last for weeks, in which case the operation might become a recovery effort drawing on the skills she has acquired as a deputy coroner for Yellowstone and Park County, Montana.

A typical day of avalanche rescue training involves hours of patient waiting in frozen conditions. One trainer hides in a snow cave or buries a piece of clothing with human scent while a second trainer takes the dogs to another area. When the dogs are released downwind a distance away, they must sniff in an organized pattern while conducting their search so that maximum ground is covered without missing an area.

"Search dogs are special animals," she says. "They are smart and determined and work hard for their reward. We can tell from puppyhood if they have what it takes to find someone—even underwater."

Being involved in search-and-rescue pulls Colette back into the wild country of Yellowstone. On a bright summer day, she and her dog may be found searching the backcountry for a missing visitor or employee. "The true gift of Yellowstone is having a place where we don't call all the shots. It belongs to nature. My job will always be to help people keep it that way."

Fifty-seven: Colette staying fit in Gardiner, Montana.

"We live the life that we offer to share with you. The wilderness is good for the soul."

Warren Johnson

Trail, fishing, and hunting guide; ecologist

When Laura Bush visited Yellowstone with friends on a vacation, there was no question about who should guide them into the park to get the best experience. Since 1979, Warren Johnson and his family's company, Hell's A-Roarin' Outfitters, have been leading horseback rides and hunting trips and guiding visitors who seek a total wilderness experience—complete with a log cabin!—along with a few essential amenities like campfires, warm beds, and a well-stocked chuck wagon.

The advance team who located Warren and his company to plan an experience for Mrs. Bush had heard not only about his lifelong experience with horses, pack mules, and adventures tailored to the interests and skills of visitors, but also his broad knowledge of animals and plant life in the park. Hunters who are guided by Warren into the wilds surrounding Yellowstone are guaranteed to return with magnificent trophies: sightings of deer, elk, bison, cougar, and more. Warren knows how to find them.

"Mrs. Bush seemed surprised that I knew 95 percent of the plants that we came upon as we walked and rode," he said. "I love nature. As a kid, as soon as my feet hit the ground in the morning, I was outside with horses and mules—and I loved every minute of it."

Warren grew up on a ranch in Jardine, Montana—a ghost town near Gardiner—on the northern border of Yellowstone. "We had two hundred horses and it was my job to help take care of them—making sure they had salt, food, and water."

Caring for animals throughout his life also led him to acquire detailed knowledge about particular indigenous plant foods that are needed by both wildlife and livestock and the dangers of invasive plant species that can destroy the natural food chain. Warren has "weed-pulling days." If he is out on one of his four-hour walks, "just for a little fresh air," he will most likely be carrying a sack in which he places the weeds as he finds them and records their location for ongoing monitoring. Some noxious invaders, such as the Russian knapweed, create an odor and taste in the ground that causes animals to avoid grazing, thus limiting their food supply.

Warren is dedicated to sharing the happiness he experiences living in and around wilderness areas. He says, "If I died right now, I'd say that my life was perfect. Fresh air and nature bring us back to who we are. Even eyesight improves!"

Outdoorsman: Warren has a long family history of guiding people into the wilderness for hunting, fishing, or just enjoying nature.

"Earthquakes shake things up. If one happens, I head for the park."

Will Boekel

Geyser gazer, student

It's 12:10 P.M. and the placard next to the reception desk in the Old Faithful Inn says that the next eruption of its namesake geyser will occur in five minutes. The crowd has moved out to the boardwalks behind the inn in front of a steaming, burbling, mostly flat area that looks like the surface of a planet far out in space, except for the grove of lodgepole pine in the background. Visitors have gathered on this spot since at least 1870, when the Washburn expedition noted the size, frequency, and regularity of this spurt of steam and water shooting as high as 184 feet in the air from a cone-shaped mound of earth and decided it was worthy of the name Old Faithful.

Close to 12:15 P.M. the crowd buzzes as the first sign of life from below the earth appears. After five minutes of 10-foot spurts and steam, an onlooker asks with disappointment, "Is that it?" Fortunately Will Boekel, geyser expert, is standing nearby. Just as he says, "Give her another minute," *whoosh,* a column of white, frothy, hot water shoots up, climbing first 50 feet and then on up to what Will estimates to be about 150 feet for two and a half minutes. The crowd goes wild. Just as quickly, the geyser retreats back to bubbles on the surface of the earth and most viewers head back to the gift shop—except for Will. He has work to do. He's entering all that he has observed into his smart phone for transmission to the Geyser Observation and Study Association, a nonprofit organization that serves as a repository for the many avid volunteer observers to record their observations of geysers and other geothermal phenomena.

Will, who also works at the front desk of the inn, comes prepared for long hours of observation with a backpack containing water and food, a jacket in case of rain, watches, a two-way radio to communicate with other "geyser gazers," and a smart phone to post eruptions to the online data base. He discovered geyser gazing and the organization in 2011 and has been hooked ever since.

"I've met fascinating people from around the world, and we are like a family."

Originally, gazers wrote their observations in private logs and shared as much as they could. Today, they report over radio networks and write in a public online notebook. Will, a student in mechanical engineering, hopes that someday he will find work related to geysers. For now, he is just happy waiting and watching.

Observer: Waiting for an eruption at Castle Geyser in Yellowstone National Park.

"I love my job and can't imagine doing anything else."

Lee Whittlesey

Yellowstone National Park historian, author

There are many unusual ways to die in Yellowstone, and Lee Whittlesey has documented them all, starting with the early days of runaway horses, drownings, and wagon accidents, to present-day bear attacks, lightning strikes, falling trees, and those unfortunate folks who mistook a crystal-clear, boiling thermal pool for something much cooler. "Danger and wilderness go hand in hand," Lee says. "That's part of the attraction of wilderness. Danger is part of the allure."

His chilling collection of true stories, *Death in Yellowstone: Accidents and Foolhardiness in the First National Park,* is a natural history of the many ways in which people can get into trouble in a place that is unsafe because it is purposefully wild. He describes how, of the more than three hundred unnatural deaths that have occurred within the Yellowstone area since 1839, most resulted from lack of knowledge, inexperience with wildlife, and simply not paying attention. "Just because a bison is wagging its tail does not mean it's happy to see you. Someone enters a wilderness area practically every day without adequate preparation for its dangers."

The convergence between people and nature is at the root of Lee's lifelong fascination with western history and Yellowstone. From the age of four, when his family traveled from Oklahoma for a family vacation, to return many times, Lee was entranced by the landscape, trout fishing, and stories of adventure—and misadventure.

Finally, a job on the back of a garbage truck at age seventeen was the start of a long, winding career through snow coach and tour bus driving, law school, graduate school in history, work as a law enforcement and interpretive ranger, and eventually, full-time park historian. "I fell in love with the history of the region because of the wilderness aspects, but it's the history of people, both known and unknown, that keeps me here. I love learning about their personalities and the towns they lived in, looking at old documents and writing about them."

Lee has more than thirty-five publications to his credit, and as a writer of history, especially the stories of people who have died in Yellowstone, he understands that each death is an intensely emotional story for someone. "I've learned about the need for a delicate, almost tender approach when a writer is required to deal with the emotions of some very good people in order to find out the facts."

And what can we learn from history in the midst of wilderness? Lee says, "Enjoy the wildness, but play safely—and think before you act."

Looking into the Past: Lee next to a wooden marker on the grave of Charlotte Forseyth in Gardiner Cemetery, which reads: "Born in about 1830."

"I love being snowed in!"

Salle Engelhardt

Yellowstone National Park interpretive ranger, artist, musician, former truck driver

Salle found her way to Yellowstone through a unique relationship with roads and maps. Born on the Tobin Bridge in Boston, on the way to the hospital at sunset, she grew up in New England. Her father, a cartographer, introduced her to the world through maps, and from a very young age she sensed that she would find her place far from her backyard.

Like many kids in the 1960s, her introduction to the West was through Yogi Bear cartoons. In the 1970s a series of jobs, from repossessing cars to truck driving, brought her to the wilds of West Yellowstone before the roads were paved. The first time she saw Yellowstone was from the cab of her cargo-filled, eighteen-wheeled semi tractor-trailer truck. "The view was breathtaking," she says. "The snowbanks were higher than my truck and I loved the idea of living someplace where I could be snowed in."

After viewing most of the country from her truck cab, she knew that Yellowstone was her favorite spot. Getting there with the right job qualifications was her next challenge. Already in her thirties, she realized she needed to get a college degree if she wished to pursue her dream. She eventually earned a master's in public administration. As part of her studies, she completed case studies on bison, the reintroduction of wolves, and the policies regarding management of snowmobiles in Yellowstone National Park.

Courageously, she sold everything she owned, moved from Idaho to West Yellowstone, and applied for a ranger position. Today, she is an expert at snowbound living as well as wolves, bears, birds, and the habitat and environs of Yellowstone.

How does she endure those long winters with more than ten feet of snow, even if she loves being snowed in? In college, she had joined a chorus and found that singing in an ensemble helped her to study complex subjects. Music has been her constant companion since age three, but harmonizing in a group connected her with others—and herself. Her performances as a classically trained vocalist and studio singer and her multimedia pieces of art inspired by walks in the woods, wild mushrooms, or a particular cloud formation might surprise visitors listening to her ranger talks about wolves.

We could say that Salle was always headed for Yellowstone, and she created a path that would get her there.

Meditation: Salle contemplates a site near West Yellowstone where twenty-eight campers died in a landslide during the 1959 earthquake.

"We should think like nature and look at the fundamentals of things. I have listened to the voice of the mountain for most of my life."

John J. Craighead

Wildlife advocate and researcher

The death of John's twin brother, Frank, at age eighty-two in 2001 marked the physical end of eight decades of almost continuous collaboration between the two. The results of their work—and their fun together over the years—survive in the dozens of articles, monographs, and documentaries they created both individually and in concert with each other. Even now, in his nineties, John continues to publish scholarly work and remains a visionary and voice of reason for the rights of animals and the conservation of nature.

No concise summary can capture the myriad of scientific contributions that were made by John Craighead and his brother in their pioneering studies of animal behavior and research methodology. As teenagers, Frank and John were fascinated with birds of prey, leading them to learn the ancient practice of falconry and to become part of a small group of enthusiasts who revived the sport in the United States. They were also the first wildlife biologists to study a species of large mammals by first observing individual animals and then applying that knowledge to the larger population.

Over five decades, both brothers pursued highly technical research that shaped public environmental policy and inspired legions of young scientists. When the National Wild and Scenic Rivers Act was passed in 1968, much of the wording came from articles written by them.

Twelve years of research by the Craighead brothers, between 1959 and 1971, also helped to save grizzly bears from extinction in the lower forty-eight states. By tracking dozens of Yellowstone bears for days on end, trapping and examining them, and sometimes following them into their dens, the brothers documented the bears' home range and diet, provided solid population estimates, and discovered that their chief cause of death was human contact. When the National Park Service decided in the 1960s to completely close the open garbage pits in Yellowstone, the Craighead brothers knew that more than half of the bear population would face imminent starvation and likely search for food in populated areas unless the dumps were phased out slowly.

Today, the family tradition of wildlife-wildland advocacy continues at the Craighead Institute in Bozeman. Younger generations of researchers continue to study John's pioneering use of radio telemetry to track and study free-ranging animals and his "mud and boots" approach to understanding nature—and the nature of wildness. John died in 2016 at age 100.

Environmentalist Extraordinaire: John in his home in Missoula, Montana, with a bear sculpture of his own creation.

"I have worked with incredible people to capture something of their lives and love of Yellowstone."

Steve Horan
Photographer

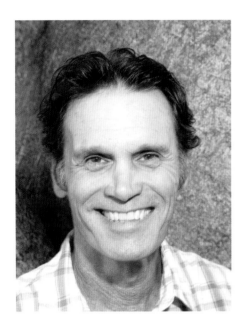

Steve Horan studied photography in Toronto and the U.S. and has worked in many aspects of the art. The *People of Yellowstone* project unites his passion for community and its connection to the natural world.

Steve spent five years crisscrossing three states to find people to photograph for this book. Every portrait was a collaboration between subject and photographer.

He has had many gallery exhibitions of his work in the U.S. and Canada.

See more of his *People of Yellowstone* portraits at **www.stevehoran.com**

"I love telling the stories of why people were drawn to live and work in Yellowstone."

Ruth W. Crocker
Essayist

Ruth W. Crocker is the author of the award-winning memoir *Those Who Remain: Remembrance and Reunion After War*. Her work has appeared in the *Gettysburg Review*, *O-Dark-Thirty*, the *Saturday Evening Post*, and *TAPS* magazine in addition to anthologies of creative nonfiction and many trade magazines. Her essays have been nominated for a Pushcart Prize and listed in Best American Essays.

Ruth was introduced to Yellowstone by her brother, ranger Bob Whipple. She says, "Bob's passion for Yellowstone was contagious. After hearing his descriptions, I had to see the place for myself and discover the stories of others who love the park."

Visit her website at **www.ruthwcrocker.com**